*As unemployment rises, the struggle, Gorz insists, is not
for the 'Right to Work' but for an income regardless of
work, for the sharing of the reduced amount of necessary
social labour, above all for the primacy of autonomous,
self-determined activity. And it is a struggle, he claims, that
is already taking place.*

New Statesman

*Gorz is also candid in confronting the challenge to conven-
tional socialist theory presented by the disappearance of an
industrial working class. This latest essay is vintage
Gorz—stimulating in its insight and rich in its documentation, but finally frustrating in the failure of the analysis to
lead to any programme of action.*

The Guardian

*Gorz's terrain is one that must be thought through. The
disastrous failure of present day Labourism to confront the
impact of technological re-equiment permits the credibility
of Thatcherism. A new socialist project must be formed
that can include the abolition of work and the liberation of
desire.*

City Limits

*...a stimulating book which addresses several of the issues
which are bound to be raised in the forthcoming inquests
on British socialism.*

New Society

*...a tightly-structured tour de force with a universal
application.*

Marxism Today

Contents

for Dorine

Preface: Nine Theses for a Future Left

This book is an essay in the fullest sense of the word. It is an attempt to outline the perspectives and the themes around which a L ft endowed with a future rather than burdened with nostalgia might re-emerge. It makes no pretence to have answered all the questions it raises.

1. Its central theme is the liberation of time and the abolition of work — a theme as old as work itself. *Work* has not always existed in the way in which it is currently understood. It came into being at the same time as capitalists and proletarians. It means an activity carried out: for someone else; in return for a wage; according to forms and time schedules laid down by the person paying the wage; and for a purpose not chosen by the worker. A market gardener 'works'; a miner growing leeks in his back garden carries out a freely chosen activity.

'Work' nowadays refers almost exclusively to activities carried out for a wage.[1] The terms 'work' and 'job' have become interchangeable: work is no longer something that one *does* but something that one *has*. One 'looks for work' and 'finds work' just as one 'looks for' or 'finds' a job.

Work is an imposition, a heterodetermined, heteronomous activity, perceived by most of those who either 'have' it or are 'looking for' it as a nondescript sale of time. One works 'at Peugeot's' or 'at Boussac's' rather than to make cars or textiles. One 'has' a good or a bad job according to how much one earns — and only secondly according to the nature of the task and its purpose. One can have a 'good' job in the armaments industry

---

1. On the origins and etymology of the word 'work', see M. Godelier, 'Work and its representations...', *History Workshop Journal*, no. 10, 1980, pp. 164-74 (translator's note).

and a 'bad' job in the health service.

For both wage earners and employers, work is only a means of earning money and not an activity that is an end in itself. Therefore work is not freedom. Of course in any sort of work, even on an assembly-line, a minimum of freely given commitment is essential. Without it, everything grinds to a halt. But this necessary minimum of freedom is, at the same time, negated and repressed by the organisation of work itself. This is why the notion that it is necessary to free ourselves *in* our work as well as *from* work, and *from* work as well as *in* our work, is as old as the waged working class itself. During the heroic age of the labour movement, the abolition of work and the abolition of wage labour were goals between which no difference was made.

2. The difference between wage labour and self-determined activity is the same as the difference between use-value and exchange-value. Work is carried out essentially for a wage — which serves to sanction the social utility of the activity in question and entitles its recipient to a quantity of social labour equivalent to that which he or she has sold. Working for a wage amounts to working in order to purchase as much time from society as a whole as it has previously received.

Self-determined activity, on the other hand, is not principally concerned with the exchange of quantities of time. It is its own end, whether it takes the form of aesthetic activity (like games, including love) or artistic creation. When self-determined activity is one of production, it is concerned with the creation of objects destined not for sale, but to be consumed or used by the producers themselves or by their friends or relatives.

The abolition of work will only be emancipatory if it also allows the development of autonomous activity.

Thus the abolition of work does not mean abolition of the need for effort, the desire for activity, the pleasure of creation, the need to cooperate with others and be of some use to the community. Instead, the abolition of work simply means the progressive, but never total, suppression of the need to purchase the right to live (which is almost synonymous with the right to a wage) by alienating our time and our lives.

The abolition of work means the freeing or liberation of time. Freeing time — so that individuals can exercise control over their bodies, their use of themselves, their choice of activity, their goals and productions — represents a demand that has been translated in a regrettably reductive way by the phrase 'the right to idleness'. The demand to 'work less' does not mean or imply the right to 'rest more', but the right to 'live more'. It means the right to do many more things for ourselves than money can buy — and even to do some of the things which money at present *can* buy.

This demand has never been more urgent than now. This is so for a number of reasons which legitimate and reinforce one another.

3. The most immediately apparent of these reasons is that the abolition of work is a process already underway and likely to accelerate. In each of the three leading industrialised nations of Western Europe, independent economic forecasts have estimated that automation will eliminate 4-5 million jobs in ten years, unless there is a sharp reduction in the number of working hours as well as in the form and purpose of productive activity. Keynes is dead. In the context of the current crisis and technological revolution it is absolutely impossible to restore full employment by quantitative economic growth.[2] The alternative rather lies in a different way of managing the abolition of work: instead of a society based on mass unemployment, a society can be built in which time has been freed.

A society based on mass unemployment is coming into being before our eyes. It consists of a growing mass of the permanently unemployed on one hand, an aristocracy of tenured workers on the other, and, between them, a proletariat of temporary workers carrying out the least skilled and most unpleasant types of work.

The outlines of a society based on the free use of time are only beginning to appear in the interstices of, and in opposition to, the present social order. Its watchword may be defined as: let us work less so that we all may work and do more things by ourselves in our free time. Socially useful labour, distributed over all those willing and able to work, will thus cease to be anyone's exclusive or leading activity. Instead, people's major occupation may be one or a number of self-defined activities, carried out not for

2. See Appendix 1 below.

money but for the interest, pleasure or benefit involved.

The manner in which the abolition of work is to be managed and socially implemented constitutes the central political issue of the coming decades.

4. The social implementation of the abolition of work requires that we put an end to the confusion that has arisen under the influence of Keynesianism between the 'right to work' and: the right to a paid job; the right to an income; the right to create use-values; the right of access to tools that offer the possibility of creating use-values.

The need to dissociate the right to an income from the 'right to a job' had already been stressed at the beginning of the second industrial revolution (that associated with taylorism). It was apparent then, as it is today, that the reduction in the number of working hours required to produce necessities called for new mechanisms of distribution independent of the laws of the market and the 'law of value'. If goods produced with a minimal expenditure of labour were to be purchased, it was necessary to supply the population with means of payment bearing no relation to the price of the hours of work they had put in. Ideas like those of Jacques Duboin in particular, concerning a social income guaranteed for life and a currency that cannot be accumulated, continue to circulate, mainly in Northern Europe.

Socialised distribution of production, according to need rather than effective demand, was for a long time one of the central demands of the Left. This is now becoming ever less the case. In itself, it can only lead to the state taking greater charge of individual lives. The right to a 'social income' (or 'social wage') for life in part abolishes 'forced wage labour' only in favour of a wage system without work. It replaces or complements, as the case may be, exploitation with welfare, while perpetuating the dependence, impotence and subordination of individuals to centralised authority. This subordination will be overcome only if the autonomous production of use-values becomes a real possibility for everyone.

Thus the division between 'Left' and 'Right' will, in the future, tend to occur less over the issue of the 'social wage' than over the right to autonomous production. The right to autonomous production is, fundamentally, the right of each grass-roots community to produce at least part of the goods and services it consumes without having to sell its labour to the owners of means of production or to buy goods and services from third parties.

The right to autonomous production presupposes the right of access to tools and their conviviality.[3] It is incompatible with private or public industrial, commercial or professional monopolies. It implies a contraction of commodity production and sale of labour power, and a concomitant extension of autonomous production based on voluntary cooperation, the exchange of services or personal activity.[4]

Autonomous production will develop in all those fields in which the use-value of time can be seen to be greater than its exchange-value. In other words, it will develop in situations in which what one can do oneself in a given period of time is worth more than what one could buy by working the equivalent period of time for a wage.

Only if it is combined with effective possibilities for autonomous production will the liberation of time point beyond the capitalist logic, wage system and market relations. Effective possibilities for autonomous production cannot exist for everyone without a policy providing adequate collective facilities for that purpose.

4a. Autonomous productive activity is not to be confused with 'housework'. As Ivan Illich has shown, the notion of housework only appeared with the development of a type of sexual division of labour specific to industrialism.[5] Industrialist civilisation has confined women in domestic activities that are not directly productive, so that men may spend all their working hours in factories and mines. As a result, women's activities in the household have ceased to be autonomous and self-determined. Women's work has become the precondition and subordinate appendage of male wage labour. Only the latter is considered

---

3. Ivan Illich uses the term 'convivial' to define tools that 'enhance the ability of people to pursue their own goals in their unique way', as against 'programmed tools', which engender predetermined actions.
4. On the importance of voluntary association in libertarian communist thought, see Claude Berger, *Marx, l'Association ouvrière, l'anti-Lénine, vers l'abolition du salariat*, Paris, Payot 1974.
5. Illich, *Shadow Work*, London, Boyars 1981.

important and essentially productive.

The notion that waged workers need to be relieved of domestic tasks, regarded as degrading and inferior, whereas waged work is supposedly 'noble': this notion is specific to capitalist ideology. The only important thing is to get paid irrespective of the purpose, meaning or nature of the job. Hence the housewife's activities are considered to be degrading and inferior, whereas the same activities performed for a wage — in a nursery, an aeroplane or a night-club — are held to be perfectly dignified and acceptable.

As the time spent working falls, leaving more free time, so heteronomously determined work tends to become secondary and autonomous activity dominant. A revolution in patterns of behaviour and a redefinition of values tend to endow domestic or family-based activities with a new dignity and lead to the abolition of the sexual division of labour. It is already underway in protestant societies. Women's liberation is not to be found in 'wages for housework',[6] but through association and cooperation between equals who, within the family or enlarged family, share all tasks both inside and outside the home and, where necessary, take turns at various tasks.

5. The abolition of work is neither acceptable nor desirable for people who identify with their work, define themselves through it and do or hope to realise themselves in their work. Thus the 'social subject' of the abolition of work will not be the stratum of skilled workers who take pride in their trade and in the real or potential power it confers on them. The main strategic goal of this social stratum, which has always been hegemonic within the organised labour movement, will remain the appropriation of work, of the work tools and of power over production. Automation will always be perceived by skilled workers as a direct attack on their class insofar as it undermines workers' class power over production and eliminates the possibility to identify with one's work (or even to identify one's work at all). Thus their major concern will be to resist automation, rather

---

6. It would lead only to the alienation of the 'housewife' being replaced by that of the domestic servant, and the 'sexual service' of the wife by that of the prostitute.

than to turn its weapons against their attackers. Protecting jobs and skills, rather than seeking to control and benefit from the way in which work is abolished, will remain the major concern of traditional trade unionism.

This is why it is bound to remain on the defensive.

The abolition of work is, on the other hand, a central objective for all those who, whatever they may have learned, find that 'their' work can never be a source of personal fulfilment or the centre of their lives — at least for as long as work remains synonymous with fixed hours, pre-planned tasks, limited competence, regularity and assiduity over months and years, and the general impossibility of being active in several fields at the same time. All those who are 'allergic to work', as Rousselet has put it, can no longer be considered to be marginals.[7] They are not part of a subculture existing on the fringes of society, but represent a real or potential majority of those in 'active employment' who see 'their' work as a tedious necessity in which it is impossible to be fully involved.

This non-involvement is largely the result of the divergent changes on the cultural level on the one hand, and of the type of skills required by the majority of jobs on the other. Jobs have tended to become 'intellectualised' — that is, to require mental rather than manual operations — without stimulating or satisfying intellectual capacities in any way. Hence the impossibility for workers to identify with 'their' work and to feel that they belong to the working class.

I have used the term 'a non-class of non-workers' to designate the stratum that experiences its work as an externally imposed obligation in which 'you waste your life to earn your living'. Its goal is the abolition of workers and work rather than their appropriation. And this prefigures the future world. The abolition of work can have no other social subject than this non-class. I do not infer from this that it is already capable of taking the process of abolishing work under its control and of producing a society based upon the liberation of time. All I am asserting is that such a society cannot be produced without, or in opposition to, this non-class, but only by it or with its support. To object that it is

---

7. Jean Rousselet, *L'allergie au travail*, Paris, Editions du Seuil 1978.

hard to see how a 'non-class' could 'seize power' is beside the point. Its obvious incapacity to seize power does not prove either that the working class *is* capable of doing so (if it were, it would be obvious) or that power should be *seized*, rather than dismantled, controlled, if not abolished altogether.

6. The definition of the 'non-class of non-workers' as the potential social subject of the abolition of work is not the result of an ethical or ideological choice. The choice is not between the abolition of work and the re-establishment of well-rounded trades in which everyone can find satisfaction. The choice is: *either* a socially controlled, emancipatory abolition of work *or* its oppressive, anti-social abolition.

It is impossible to reverse the general trend (which is at once social, economic and technological) and re-establish the old crafts for everybody's benefit, so that autonomous groups of workers may control both production and its products and find personal fulfilment in their work. Inevitably, as the process of production becomes socialised, the personal character of work is eroded. The process of socialisation implies a division of labour and a standardisation and formalisation of tools, procedures, tasks and knowledge. Even if, in accordance with recent trends, relatively small, decentralised units of production were to replace the industrial dinosaurs of the past, and even if repetitive, mindless work were abolished or (should this be impossible) distributed among the population as a whole, socially necessary labour would still never be comparable to the activities of craftsworkers or artists. It will never be a self-defined activity in which each individual or group freely determines the modalities and objectives of work and leaves its inimitable personal touch upon it. The socialisation of production inevitably implies that microprocessors or ball-bearings, sheet metals or fuels are interchangeable wherever they are produced, so that both the work and the machinery involved also have the same interchangeable characteristics everywhere.

This interchangeability is a fundamental precondition for reducing the length of working time and distributing socially necessary labour among the population as a whole. The old proposal — as old as the working-class movement itself — to reduce the number of working hours by 20 per cent by employing a corresponding proportion of additional workers implicitly presupposes that workers and work are more or less interchangeable. If 1,000 people on a 32-hour week are to do the work of 800 people working 40 hours, then the type of work must not call for irreplaceable personal skills.

Thus the depersonalisation, standardisation and division of labour constitute the prerequisites to both a reduction of working hours and its desirability. Each individual's work *can* be reduced because others are also capable of doing it, and it *should* be reduced so that each individual may do other, more personally satisfying and fulfilling things.

In other words, the heteronomous nature of work, which is the consequence of its socialisation and increased productivity, is also what makes the liberation of time and the expansion of autonomous activity both possible and desirable. It is a dangerous illusion to believe that 'workers' control' can make everyone's work gratifying, intellectually stimulating and personally fulfilling.

7. In any complex society, the nature, modalities and objectives of work are, to a large extent, determined by necessities over which individuals or groups have relatively little control. It is certainly possible to 'self-manage' workshops or to self-determine working conditions or to co-determine the design of machines and the definition of tasks. Yet as a whole these remain no less determined in a heteronomous way by the social process of production or, in other words, by society insofar as it is itself a giant machine. Workers' control (erroneously equated with workers' self-management) amounts in reality to self-determining the modalities of what has already been heteronomously determined: the workers will share and define tasks within the framework of an already existing social division of labour. They are not, however, able to define the division of labour itself nor, for example, the specifications of ball-bearings. They may eliminate the degrading characteristics of work, but they cannot endow it with the characteristics of personal creativity. What is at issue, then, is a form of alienation inherent not only in capitalist relations of production, but in the socialisation of the process of production itself: in the workings of a complex, machine-like society. The effects of this alienation can be attenuated, but never entirely eliminated.

The consequences of this situation are not entirely negative —

provided that its ineradicable reality is accepted. Above all, it must be recognised that there can never be a complete identity between individuals and their socialised work and, inversely, that socialised work cannot always be a form of personal activity in which individuals find complete fulfilment. 'Socialist morality' — with its injunction that each individual be completely committed to his or her work and equate it with personal fulfilment — is oppressive and totalitarian at root. It is a morality of accumulation, which mirrors the morality of the bourgeoisie in the heroic age of capitalism. It equates morality with love of work, while at the same time depersonalising work through the processes of industrialisation and socialisation. In other words, it calls for love of depersonalisation — or self-sacrifice. It rejects the very idea of 'the free development of each individual as the goal and precondition of the free development of all' (Marx). It sets itself against the ethic of the liberation of time which originally dominated the working-class movement.

If individuals are to be reconciled with their work, it must be recognised that, even under workers' control, work is not and should not be the centre of one's life. It should be only one point of reference. The liberation of individuals and society, together with the regression of wage labour and commodity-based relationships, requires the domination of autonomous over heteronomous activity.

8. In describing the 'non-class of non-workers' as the (potential) social subject of the abolition of work, I am not claiming to put in place the working class, as defined by Marx, another class invested with the same type of historical and social 'mission'. The working class defined by Marx or marxists derives its theological character from being perceived as a subject transcending its members. It makes history and builds society through the agency of its unwitting members, whatever their intentions. The working class thus defined is a transcendent subject by which the workers are thought in their true being; but it remains unthinkable for the workers themselves, just as our body is unthinkable for the millions of its component cells or God is unthinkable for God's creatures. This is why the working class had and still has its priests, prophets, martyrs, churches, popes and wars of religion.

The non-class of those who are recalcitrant to the sacralisation of work, on the contrary, is not a 'social subject'. It has no transcendent unity or mission, and hence no overall conception of history and society. It has, so to speak, no god or religion, no reality other than that of the people who compose it. In short, it is not a class but a non-class. For this very reason it has no prophetic aura. It is not the harbinger of a new subject-society offering integration and salvation to its individual members. Instead it reminds individuals of the need to save themselves and define a social order compatible with their goals and autonomous existence.

This is the specific characteristic of all nascent social movements. Like the peasant movement, the protestant reformation and, subsequently, the working-class movement itself, the movement formed by all those who refuse to be nothing but workers has very strong libertarian overtones. It is a negation and rejection of law and order, power and authority, in the name of the inalienable right to control one's own life.

9. Of course, this right can only be affirmed if it corresponds to a power that individuals derive from their own existence rather than their integration into society — in other words, from their own autonomy. The building up of this autonomous power is, in the present phase, the central concern of the nascent movement. Since it is a fragmented and composite movement, it is by nature refractory towards organisation, programming, the delegation of functions or its integration into an already established political force. This is at once its strength and its weakness.

It is its strength because a different kind of society, opening up new spaces of autonomy, can only emerge if individuals set out from the very beginning to invent and implement new relationships and forms of autonomy. Any change in society presupposes an extra-institutional process of cultural and ethical change. No new liberties can be granted from above, by institutionalised power, unless they have already been taken and put into practice by people themselves. In the early phase of a movement, its suspicion towards institutions and established parties is a reflection of its reluctance to pose problems in traditional ways or to accept without question that debates on the management of the state by political parties, or the management of society by the state, are the last word on anything.

It is its weakness, however, because spaces of autonomy captured from the existing social order will be marginalised, subordinated or ghettoised unless there is a full transformation and reconstruction of society, its institutions and its legal systems. It is impossible to envisage the predominance of autonomous activities over heteronomous work in a society in which the logic of commodity production, profitability and capitalist accumulation remains dominant.

The predominance of autonomous activities is thus a political matter as well as an ethical and existential choice. Its realisation presupposes not only that the movement is able to open up new spaces of autonomy through its practice, but also that society and its institutions, technologies and legal systems can be made compatible with an expanded sphere of autonomy. The process of transforming society in accordance with the aims of the movement will certainly never be an automatic effect of the expansion of the movement itself. It requires a degree of consciousness, action and will. In other words it requires politics. The fact that the post-capitalist, post-industrial, post-socialist society envisaged here[8] cannot — and should not — be as integrated, ordered and planned as preceding societies have been, does not make it possible to dispense with the problem of defining the workings, juridical bases and institutional balance of power to be found in this society. However non-integrated,

---

8. In the traditional marxist schema socialism is a transitional stage towards communism. During this transition, the development and socialisation of the productive forces is to be completed; wage labour to be retained and even extended. The abolition of wage labour (at least as the dominant form of work) and market relations is, according to the schema, to be realised with the advent of communism.

In advanced industrial societies, socialism is already historically obsolete. As was recognised in the theses of the *Manifesto* group in Italy in 1969, political tasks have now gone beyond the question of socialism, and should turn upon the question of communism as it was originally defined.

The use of these terms is made difficult by the perversion and devaluation of the notions of 'socialism' and 'communism' by regimes and parties that claim to represent them. The crisis of marxism, which is reflected in these difficulties, should not, however, lead to forsaking analysis of capitalism, socialism, their crises and what lies beyond. The conceptual apparatus of marxism is irreplaceable, and it would be as childish to reject it wholesale as to consider *Capital*, despite its unfinished and luxuriant condition, as revealed truth.

diverse, complex, pluralistic and libertarian it may be, it will still remain one among a number of possible choices of society and will have to be realised by conscious action.

I do not know what form this action will take, or which political force might be able to take it. I only know that this political force is necessary, and that its relationship with the movement will be — and should be — as strained and conflictual as was that between the (anarcho-syndicalist) trade-union movement and the political parties of the working class. The subordination of the one to the other has always led to the bureaucratic sterility of both, especially when political parties have confused politics with control of the state apparatus.

I have therefore deliberately left this question open and unresolved. In the present phase, we must dare to ask questions we cannot answer and to raise problems whose solution remains to be found.

André Gorz
December 1980

Introduction

There is a crisis in marxist thinking because a crisis has developed within the labour movement. Over the past 20 years, the link between the development of the productive forces and the growth of class antagonism has been broken. This does not mean that the internal contradictions of capitalism are not considerable. They have never been more spectacular. Capitalism has never been less able to solve the problems it has generated. Yet this inability has not been fatal. Instead capitalism has acquired a barely examined and often poorly understood capacity to manage the non-resolution of its problems. It has become able to accommodate its dysfunctions, even drawing renewed strength from this state of affairs. For the problems it has found to be insoluble are also intrinsically insoluble. They will remain so even when the political organisations of the working class come to control the mechanisms of state power. They will remain insoluble for as long as the mode, the forces and the relations of production retain their present form.

Who or what can change them? This question lies at the core of the present crisis of the marxist tradition. The tradition is based upon a number of interconnected assumptions *which will remain unverified in the future as they have been in the past.* They are:

1. The development of the forces of production will create the *material* base for the establishment of socialism.

2. The development of the forces of production will create the *social* preconditions for the establishment of socialism, in the form of a working class collectively capable of taking over and managing the forces of production whose development brought it into being.

Reality however is quite different. In fact:

1. The development of the productive forces is functional exclusively to the logic and needs of capital. Their development

will not only fail to establish the material preconditions of socialism, but are an obstacle to its realisation. The productive forces called into being by capitalist development are so profoundly tainted by their origins that they are incapable of accommodation to a socialist rationality. Should a socialist society be established, they will have to be entirely remoulded. Thus any theory assuming the continued functioning of the existing productive forces will be automatically incapable of developing or even perceiving a socialist rationality.

2. The productive forces that have developed in capitalist society do not lend themselves either to direct appropriation by the collective worker who sets them to work, or to collective appropriation by the proletariat as a whole.[1] In fact, capitalist development has produced a working class which, on the whole, is unable to take command of the means of production and whose immediate interests are not consonant with a socialist rationality.

This is the present state of affairs. Capitalism has called into being a working class (or, more loosely, a mass of wage earners) whose interests, capacities and skills are functional to the existing productive forces, which themselves are functional solely to the rationality of capital.

Thus the eradication of capitalism and its transcendence in the name of a different rationality can only come from areas of society which embody or prefigure the dissolution of all social classes, including the working class itself.

---

1. By proletariat I mean workers who, because of their position in the productive process and society as a whole, can only put an end to their exploitation and impotence by putting an end — *collectively*, as a class — to the power and domination of the bourgeois class.

By bourgeois class, I mean the collective 'functionary' of capital — all those who manage, represent and serve capital and its requirements.

1. The Working Class According to Saint Marx

Marx's theory of the proletariat is not based upon either empirical observation of class conflict or practical involvement in proletarian struggle. No amount of empirical observation or practical involvement as a militant will lead to the discovery of the historical role of the proletariat — a role which, according to Marx, constitutes its being as a class. Marx made the point many times: empirical investigation of the real condition of the proletariat will not disclose its class mission. On the contrary, only a knowledge of this mission will make it possible to discover the true being of the proletarians. Consequently it is of little importance to know what proletarians themselves think they are, and it matters little what they *believe* they are doing or expecting. All that matters is what they *are*. Even if their present behaviour is a little mystified and their current desires somewhat at odds with their historical role, sooner or later essence will out and reason will triumph over mystification. In other words, the being of the proletariat transcends the proletarians. It is a sort of transcendental guarantee that proletarians will ultimately conform to the class line.[1]

This suggests a rather obvious question. Who is in a position to know and say what the proletariat is, if proletarians themselves have only a deformed or mystified consciousness of what they truly are? Traditionally, of course, the answer has been:

---

1. I am paraphrasing *The Holy Family*, chapter 4, section IV, where Marx writes, 'It is not a question of what this or that proletarian , or even the whole proletariat, at the moment *regards* as its aim. It is a question of *what the proletariat is*, and what, in accordance with this *being*, it will historically be compelled to do. Its aim and historical action is visibly and irrevocably foreshadowed in its own life situation as well as in the whole organisation of bourgeois society today.' *Collected Works*, vol. 4, London, Lawrence & Wishart 1975, p. 37.

Marx. Marx alone was able to identify what the being and historical role of the proletariat truly *were*. Their truth is to be found in Marx's works. He is the *alpha* and the *omega*, the founder and prophet.

This answer of course is not very satisfactory. Why should Marx alone have become aware of the transcendent being of the proletariat? The question calls for a philosophical answer, but surprisingly Marx did not formulate one. We shall soon see why he could not do so.

Marx's theory of the proletariat is a striking syncretism of the three major ideological currents that informed European thought during the heroic age of the bourgeois revolutions: christianity, hegelianism and scientism. The linchpin of the system was hegelianism. Hegel had set out to show that history was a dialectical process whereby spirit (*Geist*), initially estranged from itself, becomes aware and takes possession of the world (which is only spirit existing outside and in separation from itself) and, in doing so, becomes world itself. History was seen by Hegel as a succession of stages, each one of which, because of its internal contradictions, inevitably gives birth to the following one until the whole process culminates in a synthesis which is at once the meaning of all previous history and the end of all history, its consummation.

Thus the true meaning of each stage is discernible only in the light of the final synthesis. But discernible *to whom*? Not, of course, to particular individuals responsible for a particular historical episode of whose untenable internal contradictions they are not even aware. In fact only G.W.F. Hegel was in a position to discern this meaning. For he had had the genius to see history as a process unfolding a meaning present at the end of time, from where it calls upon the multitude of its alienated, mystified, aborted and mutilated historic manifestations to transcend themselves towards it. Hegel's philosophy is christian theology translated as theophany. History is eschatology, the end of time and the reign of God, realised by the mediation of historical agents unaware of the work of transcendence which they are accomplishing. *Their* consciousness matters little because the work of history is informed by a dialectic transcending their own intentions.[2]

---

2. In *The Philosophy of Right* there is this characteristic passage: 'In an

This is the key to Marx's dialectic. He retained the principal characteristic of the hegelian dialectic: that history has a meaning which is independent of the consciousness of individuals and realises *itself*, whatever they may think, in their actions. But this meaning, instead of 'walking on its head' as spirit does in Hegel, is seen by Marx as marching on the feet of the proletariat. The labour of spirit raising the world to consciousness and ultimate unity with itself was no more than the idealist delirium of a theologian wedded to rationalism. For Marx, it is the workers, not spirit, who perform the labour of history: history is not the dialectical process of spirit taking possession of the world, but the progressive appropriation of nature by human labour. The world is not at first spirit estranged from itself but nature hostile to human life and unresponsive to human activity. Progressively however, society would be able to mould nature to its needs until, once mastery had been achieved, humanity would recognise itself in nature as its own product.

The obstacles impeding this recognition were twofold. Firstly, the power of the tools of production was still limited. Secondly, individuals were separated both from their tools of production and from the overall result of their collective labour. This separation (and resultant alienation) would only disappear with the advent of a class able to (re)produce nature as a whole by means of a totality of tools from which it would be totally alienated and which it would thus have to re-appropriate collectively. It 'would have' to and 'would be able to', according to Marx, because the means of production which had developed could not be appropriated and operated by any single individual, but only by all acting together in pursuance of a common goal. Humanity would 'recover' (in fact: create) its unity with nature when nature itself had become the work of humanity and when, by implication, the origin of humankind will be humankind itself. Communism, i.e. the advent of the proletariat as universal class, was the meaning of history.

---

examination of freedom one should not begin with the individual and individual self-consciousness but solely with the essence of self-consciousness, because, whether man realises it or not, this essence is realised through his own efforts and individuals are merely the moments of self-realisation.' *The Philosophy of Right*, Oxford, OUP 1942.

The parallel is clear. Hegel's spirit is replaced by the activity of producing the world. At first estranged and concealed from itself, this creative activity progressively emerges to self-consciousness and, as the forces of production grow in power, is led to culminate in the promethean self-affirmation of the collective worker as creator, through the universal cooperation of all, of both the world and itself. The motor of history from this perspective was not the dialectical unfolding of spirit until the end of time but the *impossibility* that an agent who actually produces the world should accept being dispossessed of the product and having the results of the work turned against the agent as means of subjection. This impossibility was both essential and historical. It would become manifest and effective only when the nature of both the techniques and social relations of production made it apparent that the world, stripped of its 'mystical veil', was the product of social labour and that individuals, divested of their 'narrow activities' — thanks to the socialisation of labour — *were* the producers of the world.

Capitalism, according to Marx, would ensure the realisation of both these conditions. As its productive forces developed, the mysterious forces of the natural world would give way to the technicised environment and manufactured wealth of the automatic factory. In its turn, this industrial universe would call forth a class whose members no longer worked with tools of their own for their narrow self-interest as individuals. They would be divested of all particular individuality and made into interchangeable workers, bringing into play a totality of immediately social capacities and technical powers in pursuance of immediately social effects.

This is what the proletariat is to be, according to Marx. With its emergence, labour would become conscious of itself as the means through which humanity and the world would be realised. History would reach its accomplishment by inaugurating the reign of a human universal. It is worth noting that this theory did not grow out of empirical observation but developed from a critical reflection, carried out in reaction to hegelianism, upon the essence of labour. For the young Marx it was not the existence of a revolutionary proletariat that justified his theory. Instead his theory enabled him to predict the inevitable emergence of the revolutionary proletariat. The analysis was governed by philosophy.

Philosophy anticipated real developments: it demonstrated that the meaning of history lay in the emergence, with the proletariat, of a universal class alone able to emancipate society as a whole. This class had to emerge if history was to be meaningful, and indeed there were already signs of the process taking place. They were however only intelligible to the philosopher *qua* philosopher. But philosophy, specific and separate consciousness of the historical mission of the proletariat, was destined to disappear as the proletariat would become conscious of its own being and translate its mission into practice. From this point philosophy would be incarnated by the proletariat itself. Philosophy was but an external consciousness of the proletariat's being; it would disappear when the proletariat reached self-consciousness. The philosophers' task was to pursue their self-suppression, i.e. the suppression of philosophy as a separate activity.

The materialist dialectic in which productive activity came to awareness of itself as the source of both humanity and the world had thus to rely on a politico-philosophical dialectic in which the proletariat came to internalise the consciousness of its being which at the outset could only exist externally in the person of Karl Marx, and subsequently in the form of the marxist-leninist vanguard.

This is where we remain. The reading of Marx outlined here is the one that generations of militants both before and after May '68 have, consciously or not, followed. Obviously it is an *historically* specific reading, drawing upon contemporary usages and points of reference and making no attempt to recover the *historical* itinerary of Marx's own thought with complete fidelity. Nonetheless, it is a *truthful* reading: one that seeks to transpose Marx's intellectual itinerary to the cultural context of the present. Like Marx, the youthful revolutionaries of the generation of May '68 have not committed themselves to the revolutionary movement and gone to work in factories *because* the proletariat acts, thinks and feels in a revolutionary way but because it *is* in itself revolutionary by destination, which is to say: it *has to be* revolutionary; it must 'become what it is'.

This philosophical stance is at the root of all that characterised the history of revolutionary movements: vanguardism, substitutionism, elitism; and their opposites: spontaneism, tailism, trade unionism. The impossibility of any empirical verification of the theory itself has kept hanging over marxism like original sin.

Being a reversal of the hegelian dialectic, the philosophy of the proletariat cannot expect its legitimation from the behaviour of empirical proletarians or from factual developments. Instead, its role is to legitimate and explain the real meaning of events. The hegelian imprint makes the philosopher into a prophet and philosophy into the revelation of the meaning of being. Hegel's followers could only be the high priests of hegelianism. They have been forgotten because they rather foolishly identified with the civil servants of the state. Marx's followers have not been forgotten, because the proletariat still keeps the mystery of its transcendence: it has not yet internalised its 'true being' nor matched its historical role; it has not yet identified with the consciousness of itself which the marxist (leninist) vanguard claims to embody. As a result the vanguard remains necessarily separate from the proletariat. And since it does remain separate, no one — least of all the proletariat — is able to arbitrate the debates dividing marxists. Since empirical verification of the theory is impossible, the various theoretical and political positions among marxists can only find legitimation in fidelity to the dogma.

Orthodoxy, dogmatism and religiosity are not therefore accidental features of marxism. They are inherent in a philosophy structured upon hegelianism (even if this structure was 'turned upon its feet'): the prophetic element it contains has no other basis than the revelation that came to the mind of the prophet himself. Any attempt to find the basis of the marxist theory of the proletariat is a waste of time.[3] All that its various protagonists can offer is reference to the work of Marx and the word of Lenin: invocation of the authority of the founders. The philosophy of the proletariat is a religion. It acknowledges as much of reality as it finds reassuring. Its examination of facts always starts from the following premise: 'given that the proletariat is and must be revolutionary, let us examine those facts which lend support to its revolutionary will and those which

---

3. What is outlined briefly here comes down to a theory of alienation of work which can certainly be found in Marx if one looks, but whose marxist legitimacy may also be disputed. See A. Gorz, *La morale de l'histoire*, Paris, Editions du Seuil 1959, chapters 2 and 3.

frustrate it.'

The terms of the problem govern the inquiry into its solution. The inquiry — and its results — would doubtless be very different if the problem were posed in the following way: 'Given that the proletariat is not revolutionary, let us examine whether it is possible that it might still become so and why it has been possible to believe that it already is.'

2. The Myth of Collective Appropriation

In marxist theory, the emergence of 'general abstract labour' at the expense of artisans' individual labour is understood to be the key to the historic necessity of communism. So long as artisans owned their tools and the products of their labour they were able to retain individual identity, leaving their mark upon what they produced and living their work as the practical expression of a certain autonomy. *Only insofar as* the products of their labour became commodities made exclusively for sale on the market was it possible for artisans to encounter the experience of alienation. They could not control the exchange-value of their products. Exchange-value depended on trade channels and circuits beyond the control of any single individual and — subsequently — upon technical innovations which only large-scale manufacture could afford. And yet despite their alienation as owners and vendors of the products of their labour, artisans continued to remain in control of work itself, as the activities of conceiving and producing, of transforming raw materials into finished artefacts, were governed by rhythms and methods which, within limits, varied from individual to individual.

Artisans were thus both able to control their own work, and alienated in their role of owners and vendors. They thus had *particular and limited interests*, amounting to a desire to maintain the highest and most stable exchange-value for whatever they produced. This objective presupposed a capacity to exercise monopoly or, when this was impossible, to league together with other artisans and to have the city restrict the numbers in particular urban trades, the length of the working day, the conditions governing the sale of goods and so on.

The conditions that allowed artisans a degree of autonomous control over their work were, at the same time, a limitation of the extent of that control. As a specialist in a particular trade an artisan was unlikely to have any interest or desire to extend that control beyond the confines of the specific trade in question. Membership of a trade implied a specific identity and a well-defined social position. As a result, artisans had an interest in defending or improving their respective social positions rather than in calling society as a whole into question or in seeking to remodel it on a new basis.

Just because they owned the tools of 'their' trades, artisans — or free labourers engaged in production for the market in the domestic system — remained prisoners of particular forms of work, of particular, even individual, skills learned and practised over a lifetime, and of specific occupational, commercial and local interests. According to Marx, their proletarianisation would free these narrow individualities from their particular limitations. Once dispossessed of their tools and trades, separated from the products of their labour and forced to carry out predetermined amounts of work involving an impersonal socialised know-how, workers would perceive themselves as the sheer universal power of general abstract labour: i.e. of labour stripped of all particular determinations to the extent that it had become the very essence of social labour, unlinked to any individual interest, private property, need for specific objects, or relationship to any product.

In other words, proletarianisation would replace particular producers and their 'limited interests' by a class of *producers in general* who would be immediately aware of their power over the world and conscious of their capacity to produce and recreate that world and humanity itself. With the advent of the proletariat, the supreme poverty of indeterminate power would be the seed of virtual omnipotence. Since proletarians have no trades, they are capable of any kind of work; since they have no particular skills, they have a universal social capacity to acquire them all; since they are not bound to any particular work or specific production, they are in a position to appropriate them all, to take over the system of industrial production of the whole world; since they have nothing, they are able to want everything and be satisfied with nothing less than the complete appropriation of all riches.

Throughout his life Marx was to reiterate this vocation of the proletarians to both being everything and being able to do everything — not only as a class but individually. The problem, which Marx and the subsequent marxist tradition had then to resolve, was how the proletarians' vocation as a class would be mirrored and enacted by proletarians individually. In his first major discussion of the problem, Marx was far from clear. He states that because they had been dispossessed of everything and stripped of their humanity, proletarians, 'in order to safeguard their very existence', *must* (Marx sometimes wrote 'must and can') recapture their humanity in its entirety and radically transform the world. Having made this initial assertion (which may also be found in his earliest philosophical writings), Marx then went on — without further explanation — to make a second assertion, which has very different implications. *Because* they are nothing, he wrote, 'proletarians of the present day are *in a position*' to become everything, both collectively and — above all — individually. Here is the whole section:

> Thus things have now come to such a pass that the individuals must appropriate the existing totality of productive forces, not only to achieve self-activity, but, also, merely to safeguard their very existence.
>
> This appropriation is first determined by the object to be appropriated, the productive forces, which have been developed to a totality and which only exist within a universal intercourse... The appropriation of these forces is itself nothing more than the development of the individual capacities corresponding to the material instruments of production. The appropriation of a totality of instruments of production is, for this very reason, the development of a totality of capacities in the individuals themselves.
>
> This appropriation is further determined by the persons appropriating. Only the proletarians of the present day, who are completely shut off from all self-activity, are in a position to achieve a complete and no longer restricted self-activity, which consists in the appropriation of a totality of productive forces and in the development of a totality of capacities entailed by this.[1]

How was it possible for Marx to move from asserting an

---

1. K. Marx, *The German Ideology*, in *Collected Works*, vol. 5, London, Lawrence & Wishart 1976, p. 87.

objective necessity ('individuals must appropriate the existing totality of productive forces to safeguard their very existence') to the assertion of an existential capacity: 'only the proletarians of the present day are in a position to achieve a complete and no longer restricted self-activity... in the development of a totality of capacities'? There is no answer to the question. The problem of the *capacity* of the proletariat to become everything in each of its members is not of the same order as the problem of the *necessity* for the appropriation of everything. The former belongs to philosophy. It was extrapolated from the concept of the essence of the proletariat as the universal power of labour bringing itself to self-consciousness as the origin of the world and history which Marx derived from Hegel. The assertion of the necessity for the appropriation of everything, on the other hand, was the result (or apparent result) of an analysis of the historical process of proletarianisation. This analysis was not, however, able to establish any basis for the initial, philosophical, postulate.

Closer examination makes the following point clear: Marx's initial (philosophical) conviction was that the proletariat as a whole and each proletarian in particular must *be able* to take control of the totality of productive forces in order to develop the totality of its capacities. This was a necessity if the proletariat was to stand up to its essence. Subsequent analysis of the historical process was carried out in the light of the initial conviction. Marx described the process of proletarianisation in such a way as to show that it would produce a proletariat conscious of its being, that is to say, forced by vital necessity to become what it is to be. The historical analysis was so weak, however, that it was incapable of factually supporting the thesis it was designed to underpin. At his conclusion, Marx had returned to his point of departure and had failed to develop an analysis which substantially enriched his initial intuition.

This occurred because, at the time it was developed, there was no factual evidence to support the initial idea. The majority of the proletariat consisted of dispossessed peasants and artisans. Work in the manufactures, mines and workshops was carried out mainly by women and children. Adam Smith drew attention to the fact that many manufacturers preferred to employ 'semi-imbeciles' and in *Capital* Marx himself described work in manufactures and in so-called automatic factories as a mutilation of the physical and mental faculties of workers. Factories produced 'monsters', individuals 'incapable of any independent act', 'stunted' and 'crippled' people, governed by 'an entirely military discipline'[2] — in short, factories produced the opposite of the ideal proletarian able to master 'a totality of productive forces' and find complete personal fulfilment in 'no longer restricted self-activity' (*The German Ideology*).

Only some ten years after the publication of *The German Ideology*, when faced with the presence of a new stratum of skilled and polyvalent workers who were to become the protagonists of anarcho-syndicalism, did Marx, in the *Grundrisse*, think it possible to discover the material foundation of the proletarian capacity of self-emancipation and self-management. He anticipated a process in which the development of the productive forces would result in the replacement of the army of unskilled workers and labourers — and the conditions of military discipline in which they worked — by a class of polytechnic, manually and intellectually skilled workers who would have a comprehensive understanding of the entire work process, control complex technical systems and move with ease from one type of work to another. The despotism of the factory, the officers and sergeants of production would disappear. Even the bosses would come to be seen as superfluous parasites and the moment would come when 'the associated producers' would run both the factories and society:

> Capital's ceaseless striving towards the general form of wealth drives labour beyond the limits of its natural paltriness and thus creates the material elements for the development of the rich individuality which is as all-

---

2. *Capital*, vol. 1, Harmondsworth, Penguin 1970, chapters 8 and 9 *passim*. Cf. p. 483: 'In manufacture, the social productive power of the collective worker, hence of capital, is enriched through the impoverishment of the worker in individual productive power.' And Marx goes on to cite this admirable commentary in Ferguson's *History of Civil Society*: 'Ignorance is the mother of industry as well as of superstition. Reflection and fancy are subject to err; but a habit of moving a hand or foot is independent of either. Manufactures, accordingly, prosper most where the mind is least consulted, and where the workshop may... be considered as an engine, the parts of which are men.'

sided in its production as in its consumption, and whose labour also therefore appears no longer as labour, but as the full development of activity itself, in which natural necessity in its direct form has disappeared; because a historically created need has taken the place of the natural one.[3]

Marx took up this theme on several occasions, notably in the *Critique of the Gotha Programme*. He was convinced that the figure of the polytechnic worker embodied the reconciliation of the individual proletarian with the proletariat, a flesh-and-blood incarnation of the historical subject. He was wrong. So too have been all those who have thought that the refinement and automation of production technology would lead to the elimination of unskilled work, leaving only a mass of relatively highly skilled technical workers, capable by their comprehensive understanding of technico-economic processes of taking production under their own control.[4]

We know now that exactly the opposite has occurred. Automation and computerisation have eliminated most skills and possibilities for initiative and are in the process of replacing what remains of the skilled labour force (whether blue or white collar) by a new type of unskilled worker.[5] The age of the skilled workers, with their power in the factory and their anarcho-syndicalist projects, has now to be seen as but an interlude which taylorism, 'scientific work organisation', and, finally, computers and robots will have brought to a close.

More than anyone anticipated, capital has succeeded in reducing workers' power in the productive process. It has been able to combine a gigantic increase in productive power with the destruction of workers' autonomy. It has been able to entrust ever more complex and powerful mechanised processes to the care of workers with ever more limited capacities. It has succeeded to the extent that those who were once called upon to take

3. *Grundrisse*, Harmondsworth, Penguin 1973, p. 325. (See also pp. 312-13, 387-88, 599-600 of the German edition, Berlin 1953.)
4. Notably by Radovan Richta, Serge Mallet and myself in *Strategy for Labor*, Boston, Beacon Press 1966, chapter 4.
5. See CFDT, *Les Dégâts du Progrès*, Paris, Editions du Seuil 1977.

command of the giant machinery of modern industry have been dominated by — and in — the work of domination which they were to accomplish. It has simultaneously increased the technical power and capacities of the proletariat as a whole and the impotence of proletarians themselves, whether as individuals, teams or work groups.[6]

Both the unity of the proletariat and the nature of work as the source of its universal power now lie outside and beyond the consciousness of proletarians. The *collective* power of a class able to produce the world and its history has not been transformed into a subject conscious of itself in each of its individual members. The class that collectively is responsible for developing and operating the totality of the productive forces is unable to appropriate or subordinate this totality to its own ends by recognising it as the totality of its own means. In a word the collective worker remains external to the living workers. Capitalist development has endowed the collective worker with a structure that makes it impossible for real, flesh-and-blood workers either to recognise themselves in it, to identify with it or to internalise it as their own reality and potential power.

This has happened because the collective worker, structured by the capitalist division of labour and adapted to the inert requirements of the machinery it serves, has come to function like a machine, just as armies do. From the very beginning the language of industry has been a military language:

> The technical subordination of the workman to the uniform motion of the instruments of labour, and the peculiar composition of the body of workpeople, consisting as it does of individuals of both sexes and of all ages, give rise to a barrack discipline, which is elaborated into a complete system in the factory, and brings the previously mentioned labour of superin-

---

6. Cf. *Capital*, *op. cit.* vol.1, pp. 547-8: 'The life-long speciality of handling the same tool, now becomes the life-long speciality of serving the same machine... In handicrafts and manufacture, the worker makes use of a tool; in the factory, the machine makes use of him. There the movements of the instrument of labour proceed from him, here it is the movements of the machine that he must follow [thus becoming the mere] living appendage... of a lifeless mechanism.'

tendence to its fullest development, thereby dividing
the workers into manual labourers and overseers, into
the private soldiers and N.C.O.s of an industrial
army.'[7]

The specific characteristic of an army is, however, that each
unit and group of units is wholly external to the individual
soldier. Like 'the attacking force of a cavalry squadron' or the
'defensive force of an infantry regiment', the force of the collective worker belongs to no one.[8] Worse, the organisational structure of the collective worker, devised and created from the
outside as it has been, is no more manageable or controllable for
individuals or groups of workers than an army's plan of campaign is manageable for the members of a military squad.

Thus proletarians both are and are not the collective worker,
just as soldiers both are and are not the army which manoeuvres,
advances in a pincer movement and breaks through in a surprise
attack. They *are* an army in the eyes of the general officer in
command, whose strategic plan is then broken down into hundreds of separate orders and instructions to hundreds of commanders of smaller units. Seen from the summit, an army
resembles an intelligent animal with a single head, commanding
thousands of arms and legs. But the animal does not exist for
itself. The unit commanders and individual soldiers are ignorant
of both the overall strategic plan and the entire movement of the
army. All that they know are the orders and local, partial
movements whose overall meaning escapes them.

Just as soldiers are unable to internalise the 'collective
soldier', which is the army (whatever the goals to which it might
be put), and subordinate its operations to their comman will,
neither can workers internalise the collective worker and subordinate the social process of production to their control. The
obstacle (to which we will return) is not the hierarchical structure
of the collective worker in itself, but those elements which make
such a hierarchy necessary: namely the scale of productive units,
their interdependence, and the technical, social and regional
division of labour they embody. In short, it is impossible to see

7. *ibid*. p. 549.
8. *ibid*.

the overall process in its entirety and to get the overall goal that is built into the workings of this gigantic machinery internalised by each individual and reflected in everyone's work. And this impossibility has, of course, been deliberately created in order to guarantee capitalist domination.[9]

The externality and exteriority of the collective worker in relation to particular workers is thus inherent in the material structure of the productive apparatus and in the nature of the physical processes it governs. The fact that Lenin was an enthusiast of taylorism, and Trotsky (when in power) a partisan of the militarisation of labour was not just the result of specific historical circumstances. In their eyes, there was nothing incompatible between a hierarchical and highly fragmented division of labour and the undiluted power of the proletariat, so accustomed were they to thinking of the proletariat as something entirely distinct (to the point of being separate) from proletarians themselves.

Indeed, marxist theory has never been particularly clear about *who* precisely was to carry out the collective appropriation of the means of production, or about what, where and by whom the emancipatory power conquered by the working class was to be exercised. It has also never defined the nature of the political mediations able to endow social cooperation with its voluntary character. Neither has it identified the relationship between individual workers and the collective worker, or between proletarians and the proletariat. Marx dealt with these matters only in philosophical terms in his early writings. And on that level they could appear to be soluble, at least in principle. All that was required was to treat the proletariat as an entity existing in and for itself, in the manner of Hegel's spirit, and to assume that the internalisation of its alienated being (i.e. of productive social labour) constituted the 'development of the real'. But in doing so, it was only too possible to fall into the same trap as Hegel had done by equating the Prussian state with the end of history. It was only too easy to confuse the state *as defined by the theoreticians of the proletariat* with the class power *of proletarians*, and to mistake the institutionalisation by law of the

---

9. See the quotation from Ferguson in footnote 2.

collective worker for the collective appropriation of the means of production by the producers themselves.[10]

No wonder that the ideology of self-proclaimed socialist societies has been dominated by an almost mystical cult of the proletariat, work and production, forming three externalised and separate entities. The ideology of the relationship between individuals and a society entirely subordinated to the state is more akin to the ideology of the bee-hive (i.e. of hyper-organicism, in which individual activity is controlled through a transcendent intelligence) or to military ideologies than to communism. This does not necessarily mean that this type of ideology has no proletarian or marxist undertones. Marx, and to a greater extent Engels, was fascinated by the quasi-military hierarchy of large factories. The military virtues of discipline, rectitude, self-sacrifice, abnegation and loyalty to leadership very rapidly came to dominate the internal life of those workers' organisations which claimed allegiance to marxism. Their leaders presented themselves as functionaries of the proletariat — in the same sense as Hegel had written of functionaries of the universal or Marx of the functionaries of capital — and portrayed the proletariat itself as a mystical entity to which proletarians could only expect to have the same type of relationship as soldiers to an army: that of *service and duty*.

The persistence and universality of an ideology centred upon the notions of service to production, the revolution, the proletarian state or the people cannot be explained solely in terms of historically specific deviations from the classical marxist tradition or in terms of gaps in marxist theory and the legacy of hegelianism. What needs to be explained is why these gaps and that legacy have had such influence for so long. Closer

---

10. In France the decisive step in this direction was taken by the version of marxism associated with structuralism. It was sufficient to assert that the proletariat *was not a subject* and could not become one, and that the proletarian person was not a concept and could not therefore have any status for philosophical inquiry, for it to be possible to conclude that working-class power had nothing whatsoever to do with the everyday experience of ordinary workers or communism with people's happiness. Thus any philosophical critique of stalinism was made impossible and the way opened to theoretical acceptance of state dictatorship by the collective labourer over real working people and of a state police claiming to represent the proletariat over real proletarians.

examination indicates that an explanation is already there in front of our eyes. The proletariat itself, which *is* part and parcel of the 'collective worker', mirrors the social organisation of the means of production which it sets to work. These means of production are not merely neutral mechanical devices. They embody capitalist relations of domination and exercise their command over working people in the form of inflexible technical requirements. The fact that the entire productive machine requires a quasi-military hierarchical set of relationships and a substantial body of staff officers and quartermasters means that the working-class movement is confronted by the following alternatives:

Either it holds to a productivist ideology in which the development of the productive forces is seen as the essential precondition of freedom. There is then no possibility of calling the productive forces developed by capitalism into question. All that matters is to manage and use them more efficiently and even accelerate their rate of development. Consequently the collective appropriation of the means of production can only amount to this: workers will be called upon to submit voluntarily to necessities and requirements of social production which previously they had only endured. They will thus legitimate, through the mediation of their institutional representative, the quasi-military organisational structures required by the process of production. Working-class power will consist of power over working people exercised in the name of their class.

Or the movement accepts that the means of production and a considerable part of what is actually produced do not lend themselves to real and concrete collective appropriation by real proletarians. Then the problem will be that of changing the means and structure of production in such a way as to make them collectively appropriatable. That, however, is neither an easy nor an immediately achievable task. It needs to be undertaken by the collective worker *as formed* by the development of capitalist forces of production. This requires some sort of internal modification of the working class, as well as the redefinition of skills, qualifications, responsibilities and the division of labour as a whole in the light of essentially political and cultural criteria. It presupposes that, instead of being a sort of negative imprint of the process of production, the working class is able to see it in perspective and redefine it according to its own autonomous goals. The political power of the working class has to be seen as one prerequisite among many in the transformations to be undertaken, rather than as a solution in itself.

3. The Proletariat as Replica of Capital

The process of proletarianisation is complete when workers have been stripped of all autonomous capacity to produce their own means of subsistence. For as long as workers own a set of tools enabling them to produce for their own needs, or a plot of land to grow some vegetables, and keep a few chickens, the fact of proletarianisation will be felt to be accidental and reversible. For ordinary experience will continue to suggest the possibility of independence: workers will continue to dream of setting themselves up on their own, of buying an old farm with their savings or of making things for their own needs after they retire. In short, 'real life' lies outside your life as a worker, and being a proletarian is but a temporary misfortune to be endured until something better turns up.

However limited it might be, this type of practical autonomy and the dreams (and generally unrealisable projects) of an 'independent existence' which it allows, are a bar to 'class consciousness': they preclude conscious identification with the proletariat as the inescapable social fate of each of its members. This is why, especially in Britain and Germany, the bourgeoisie — whether consciously or not — has preserved those marginal zones of autonomy formed by tiny allotments or back-yards of workers' houses. This is also why proletarian militants have generally opposed the yearning for individual autonomy, and dismissed it as a residual sign of petty-bourgeois individualism. Autonomy is not a proletarian value. The desire for autonomy has habitually been understood as either a form of regressive nostalgia or a myth which obscures the fact that the existence of a proletariat is essential to capitalism and there can be no way back to the spinning wheel or the windmill. Any proletarian seeking to escape the general condition by individual means is undermining the collective capacity of the proletariat as a whole to overthrow the bourgeoisie and collectively put an end to class society.

The political imperatives of the class struggle have thus prevented the labour movement from examining the desire for autonomy as a *specifically existential* demand.

The fact that this demand might be politically embarrassing has no bearing at all upon its irreducible reality. Needs may exist for other than political reasons and continue to exist in spite of countervailing political imperatives. This is true of certain existential needs (of an aesthetic, erotic, cultural or emotional sort) and is most particularly true of the need for autonomy. If one fails to recognise the relative autonomy of existential needs, seeking instead to subordinate them to political imperatives, every trace of them will be continually repressed as tantamount to political deviation or outright betrayal.

Repression of this sort is as old as the political and industrial class organisations of a proletariat stripped of its capacities for autonomous work. It existed well before Stalin and it has continued to exist since his time. It has its roots in the impossibility to experience being a proletarian and, even more, the unity of the proletariat, as something individually gratifying and liberating. The being of the class precedes its individual realisation since it is nothing but a set of insuperable limits imposed by the social system on the existence of proletarians. One is never free as a member of a certain class, but only *within the limits* of a class fate which one accomplishes even in the very act of seeking to escape it. The specific class being of the proletarian rests in the fact of being exploited as infinitely interchangeable labour power. Consequently, it is not as person that a proletarian is susceptible to exercise any leverage upon his or her exploiters, but only as an infinitely interchangeable being — that is to say, as an 'other' among so many nameless and totally alienated others. Being a proletarian implies that the only weapon you can turn against your exploiters is this very quantity of interchangeable work and working power into which they have made you. The ideal militant is therefore the person most able to internalise this situation. He or she no longer exists as an autonomous individuality but is, instead, the impersonal representative of a class which, as we have seen, cannot, by definition, be the subject of its own identity. The ideal militant must therefore repress his or her subjectivity and become the objective mouthpiece of the class thinking through him or her. Rigidity, dogmatism, wooden language and authoritarianism are inherent qualities of such impersonal thinking devoid of subjectivity.

Like any clergy's, this way of thinking is a reflection and extension of a religious and eschatological faith: the end of history will be a new beginning and the first will be the last. Nothing will turn into Everything. Since the proletarians have been totally negated by a social system based upon their alienation, their dispossession and self-denial of their individuality will enable them to recover as a class all that has been alienated from them. They must, in other words, lose themselves as individuals to become the masters, as a class, of the system which alienates them. *Reappropriation* (a marxist concept which has lent itself to any number of statist perversions) of this system, which dispossesses and flattens the individuals, is possible only to individuals who give up being anything by themselves so as to become everything as collective agents of the process that produces them. The class as a unit is the imaginary subject who performs the reappropriation of the system; but it is a subject external and transcendent to any individual and to all existing proletarians.[1]

The power of the proletariat is the symmetrical inverse of the power of capital. There is nothing surprising in this. Marx produced a fine demonstration of how the bourgeois is alienated by 'his' capital: he is the latter's 'functionary'. Well, the proletarian will in the same way be alienated by the proletariat when it 'collectively appropriates' capital.[2]

Thus the traditional ideology of the labour movement confirms, extends, and even completes the work begun by capital of destroying all autonomous capacities and possibilities among proletarians. The true proletarian performs but purely heteronomous work, which by itself is work completely devoid of usefulness unless it is combined with that of a large number of other

---

1. As one can see, this type of subject, with whose aura the figures of the leader, the supreme guide or the monarch are invested, has the same structure as God.
2. It might be said that it would no longer be the *same* capital because it would no longer belong to competing private owners. It would indeed belong to a single, abstract collective owner. But since when has monopoly capital not been capital?

workers. Work, in this form, has been *completely socialised*. Whatever the techniques and skills involved, they have no use-value at all for the individual worker. They cannot be put to any personal, domestic or private end.

Proletarians thus work exclusively for society. They are the suppliers of general abstract labour and, consequently, they have to buy all the concrete goods and services they consume. The totally alienated form of their work is matched by the fact that all their material needs express themselves as needs for commodities: that is needs to buy, needs for money. Everything that proletarians consume has to be bought and everything they produce is to be sold. No visible link connects consumption with production or the goods bought with the work performed.

Because of this absence of visible links it makes no difference to proletarians what they produce or what they work for. They have been stripped of all autonomous capacities by capital and compelled to work 'with the immutable regularity of a giant automaton'. Mechanisation has given rise to the fragmentation and dequalification of work and made it possible to measure work according to purely quantitative standards. You can do your job and not bother about what happens, since the quality of your work and of the finished product depends on the machines, not on you. The entire manufacturing process has been thought out once and for all by specialists whose technical intelligence is embodied in the organisation of the workshop. The very meaning of the notion of work is changed. It is no longer the workers who work the machines and adjust their actions and movements to obtain the desired result; rather they are being worked on by the machinery. The result of their labour is already there, rigorously programmed, expecting to be produced; the machine is pre-set, requiring a succession of simple regular motions. The mechanised system does the work; you merely lend it your body, your brains and your time in order to get the work done.

This is the situation: work now exists outside the worker, reified to the extent of becoming an inorganic process. Workers are there and fall in with the work that *is done*. They do not *do it* themselves. The indeterminate nature of work entails an attitude of indifference. All that matters is the wage-packet at the end of the week or month — especially since they don't ask anything else of one, no decisions or initiative. They built the system in which everyone is a cog, turned by the cog on the left and turning the one on the right. So, nothing for free: do what they tell you, and they can sort out the rest. In this way, any worker, employee or civil servant can take a malicious pleasure in rigidly adhering to the hierarchical rules and turning their work against the goals it is supposed to serve. One thinks of the French hospital worker refusing to admit an unconscious man delivered in a taxi rather than an ambulance; it is the attitude of all the public employees who avenge themselves on the public for the hierarchic oppression they endure by refusing to do or say or know anything outside their specific duties; or of the famous British example of the woodworkers' union refusing to let metal workers screw down some hoardings, while the metal workers disputed the right of the woodworker to screw boards onto metal; or of all those who stop work as soon as the siren goes, no matter how much waste and damage is caused.

This sort of resentment is the only form of freedom left to proletarians in 'their' work. They're expected to be passive? Well then, let's be passive. Or more exactly, let us use passivity as a weapon against those who imposed it. Since 'their' aim is to create passive activity, workers will respond with active passivity. This behaviour of resentment which, by overacting the role the worker is expected to play, robs the oppressors of the desired results of their orders, is the last refuge of 'working-class dignity': I'll be like you wanted, and in that way I'll get away from you. 'Screw the Bosses!' 'The Gaffer can sort it out!' 'What about our bread!' 'Shit work for shit wages!' The language of proletarian resentment is also the language of impotence.

It is all a far cry from 'the abolition of wage slavery' and 'the associated producers who subordinate nature to their collective control'. The negation of capital's negation of the worker has not taken place: there is no affirmation. We are left in a one-dimensional universe. In its struggle with capital, the proletariat takes on the identity capital itself has given it. Rather than internalising their complete dispossession and setting out to construct the universal proletarian society on the ruins of the bourgeois order, proletarians have internalised their dispossession in order to affirm their complete dependence and their need to be taken charge of completely. Since everything has been wrested from them, everything should be given to them. Since they have no power, everything should be provided by those with power. Since their work is of use to society but not to themselves, society should meet all their needs and pay a wage for every kind of work. Instead of demanding the abolition of wage labour, the proletariat has come to demand the abolition of all unwaged work.[3]

Working-class demands have turned into consumerist mass demands. An atomised, serialised mass of proletarians demand *to be given* by society, or more precisely the state, what they are unable to take or produce. The working-class struggle for power is reduced to mass mobilisations designed to bring representatives of the labour movement into power. The dictatorship of the proletariat as a transitional phase in the construction of communism is reduced to the welfare state taking care of working-class needs. The vision of 'power to the people' and 'socialism' is replaced by a political concept in which the state is everything and society nothing, where an atomised mass of proletarians, still entirely dispossessed of their own being, is patronised by the parties that run the government and turn into the mouthpiece of government itself. Parties of this sort no longer translate popular into political demands and actions but rather convey to the masses the necessities of government and the technocratic imperatives of the centralised state.

---

3. The height of alienation is reached when it becomes impossible to conceive that an activity should have a goal other than its wage or be grounded upon other than market relations. A section of the European feminist movement has taken this course by demanding a social wage for household labour. Following the strict logic of the capitalist market, such women thereby call for their *proletarianisation* as an advance over *slavery*. They refuse to *serve* the male, and demand state-paid remuneration as the means by which their labour may be recognised as a service to society as a whole, not just to the husband.

The logical conclusion of this argument is that professional prostitution is an advance over the traditional couple, and that women's liberation requires the transfer of all family-based tasks to the public services. Emancipation will be consummated only when the full-scale statisation of relations has eliminated the family as the last vestige of civil society.

This line of demands obviously conflicts with the struggle to redefine relations within the couple and to achieve a balanced, freely chosen distribution of household tasks between equal male and female partners.

It is difficult to see how things could be otherwise in a society in which the development of the productive forces has ensured that every activity is socialised and thereby fragmented, rationalised, technicised and articulated with other activities through the mediation of the state apparatus. No consumption, production, communication, transportation, illness, health care, death, learning or exchange occurs without the intervention of centralised administrations or professional agencies. The concentration of capital has destroyed the social fabric at its roots by destroying every possibility of autonomous production, consumption and exchange, whether for individuals, groups or communities.

No one produces what they consume or consumes what they produce. No productive unit — even if controlled by the 'associated producers' — produces, or is able to produce according to the needs or desires of the local population. No city — even if its inhabitants were to organise into a commune — is capable of manufacturing the things necessary to cover its vital needs or of obtaining its food through exchange with the surrounding rural communities. The division of labour now exists at transnational levels. Product lines and the location and size of factories are determined by calculations of overall profitability. Certain components are produced in certain amounts in one place to be combined a hundred miles away with other components produced in another factory and give birth to a finished product distributed over a whole continent. The same type of quasi-military staff found on factory level coordinates the activities of different factories, managing the flow of their semi-finished products, the sale of the finished products, the financing of exports and stocks, the adjustment of demand to supply and so on.

Nowhere in all of this does any worker or workers' collective experience reciprocal exchange or cooperation towards a result viewed as useful by all concerned. Instead, every worker encounters his or her dependence upon the state at every level: for supplies of vital goods, for the purchasing power of the wage, for security of employment, the length of the working week, housing, transport etc.

Thus the spontaneous reflex of the working class is to demand that this dependence upon the state be matched by duties of the state vis-à-vis the working people. Since the working class can do nothing for itself, it follows that the state should do everything for the working class. Since it has an absolute need of the state, the state ought to recognise the class an absolute right. The seizure of state power by the working class is replaced by state protection for the working class. Anything lying between the class and the state tends to be abolished. It will be an easy process since the political mediations, the institutions particular to civil society in the Gramscian sense, the fabric of social relationships and autonomous channels of communication have already been emptied of all content by monopoly capitalism.

The monopoly capitalist state can no longer be considered — as the traditional bourgeois state once was — to be an emanation of the power exercised by the bourgeoisie *within* civil society (at the level of the relations of production and exchange, of ideology and cultural models, the values of family and interpersonal relations). It is no longer possible to think of this sort of power *running from* society to local political institutions under the legitimating guise of electoral representation. Instead, the monopoly capitalist state, like monopoly capital itself, is an autonomised apparatus of domination and administration, whose unrestricted power *runs down* towards a dislocated society which it endeavours to restructure according to the requirements of capital. Through the sheer size and concentration of its economic units, capital is no longer subject to the influence and control of its juridical owners and, having broken the framework of bourgeois law, now requires centralised state regulation and possibly (although not necessarily) state ownership as conditions of its scientific management.

There is no room or flexibility in this dislocated society for the mutual adjustment between decentralised local initiatives running upwards and centralised state proposals running downwards. As a result, local political life no longer exists and, because of its absence, there are no political movements capable of carrying out a democratisation of either state or society. 'Political life' has been reduced to orchestrated debates centred upon how to exercise centralised authority and manage the government. Debates of this type necessarily set those who control the state against those aspiring to do so, while the rest of the population are consigned by both sides to the role of 'supporters'. They are thus invited to choose between the domination of state monopoly capitalism and the all-pervading domination of the monopoly of state capitalism. Lenin was right in indicating that the line separating state monopoly capitalism from state capitalism was a narrow one: the latter is nothing more than the completion — on the ruins of civil society — of the process of subordination of society to the state carried out by the former. Once completed, the process serves only to rationalise and perpetuate in a higher form those capitalist relations of production which the seizure of power by the working class was supposed to bring to an end.

If things are to develop otherwise, then there must be a radical rupture. And if there is to be a rupture, then the working class must act as a force refusing, along with its class being, to accept the matrix of capitalist relations of production of which· this being bears the imprint. But how will it acquire the capacity to undertake this negation of itself? This is a question which marxism as a 'positive science' cannot possibly answer. If the working class is what it is, if its class being is positive, then it can only cease to be what capital has made it through a rupture in the structure of capital itself. This rupture will give rise to a new structure and thereby engender a transformed working class. This has been the type of structural-determinist conception put forward by Maurice Godelier among others. It contains no room for any idea of the proletariat negating itself or any notion of the liberation and sovereignty of the associated producers. Instead, it merely posits a change of one positive being into another, without any possibility for this change (the transition from capitalism to communism) to be the result of an action carried out consciously by 'individuals pursuing their own ends'.

Marx's vision was initially a quite different one. The proletariat was to be capable of negating itself because its class being was really a negativity disguised as positivity. The proletariat was defined as the universal and sovereign producer *negated by capital*, dispossessed of its own product and reality. Only because the class being of the proletariat was negation was it possible for the act by which it negated this being to be an act of sovereign affirmation: its own emancipation.

This initial vision, which still occupied a central position in *The German Ideology*, was never properly defined or developed by Marx himself. To do so, it would have been necessary to develop a critical phenomenology of proletarian alienation, showing how workers are negated in their individual and social lives in a way which conceals from them the negativity of their class being and the possible positivity of negating that being; showing in other words that workers could only be themselves by negating what they are as proletarians.

Although the *possibility* of such an act of negation exists *ontologically* in Marx (as also in Sartre), it does not necessarily exist in cultural terms. Workers' capacity to recognise the difference between their objective position as cogs in the productive machine and their latent potential as an association of sovereign producers is not inherent in the proletarian condition.

The question is under what circumstances this capacity is likely to emerge and develop. Up to now, marxist theory has been unable to produce an answer to this problem. Worse, its predictions have been belied by the facts.

4. Workers' Power?

Sooner or later, according to marxist theory, the proletariat is to become conscious of its being as both labour power and collective productive worker. According to Marx, this means that it embodies humanity's capacity to produce very much more than what it requires for subsistence. For Marx, it lies in the essence of the productive power of the proletariat to be capable of producing more than the mere necessities of life: it is inherently capable of producing a *surplus* and supplying quantities of surplus labour uncalled for by any natural necessity or overriding need. Thus it foreshadows the future advent, beyond the realm of necessity, of the reign of freedom in which work will be an end in itself. Its goals and products will transcend the vital necessities and will reveal to the producer (the worker) her or his potentially sovereign creativeness.

The contradiction will then become intolerable between the purpose of work — which is to produce the non-necessary — and the condition of the proletarians who remain prisoners of the sphere of the necessary by having to sell their labour power for a mere subsistence wage. Sooner or later the proletariat must come to recognise that it holds the key to the realm of freedom in its own hands. For freedom to reign, all that is needed is for proletarians to unite and to take the immense productive force of industry under their control. This moment of revolutionary consciousness will be hastened by the ever more serious crises experienced by an (exploitative) system which pays a subsistence wage to the producers of a growing surplus.

In fact the moment of revolutionary consciousness did not materialise as expected. With the exception of certain limited sections of the class and on limited occasions, the proletariat has not, and does not, perceive itself as the sovereign agent of the free creation of wealth. The contradiction between its subjugation to the realm of necessity and the fact that this sphere has already been transcended by the *gratuitousness* (the non-necessity, the non-utility) of the wealth produced, has not been as widely recognised as, in theory, it should have been.

The reason may be found in the fact that the bourgeoisie succeeded in destroying at root what consciousness the proletariat might have had of its sovereign creativeness. For this purpose, eighteenth-century bosses and present-day scientific management have been applying the same recipe: they organised the work process in such a way as to make it impossible for the worker to experience work as a potentially creative activity. The fragmentation of work, taylorism, scientific management and, finally, automation have succeeded in abolishing the trades and the skilled workers whose 'pride in a job well done' was indicative of a certain consciousness of their practical sovereignty.

The idea of a subject-class of united producers capable of seizing power had been specific to these skilled workers proud of their trade. To them, power was not something abstract but a matter of daily experience: on the factory floor, power was theirs, they ruled over production. Their irreplaceable skills and practical know-how placed them at the top of a factory hierarchy that was the inverse of the social hierarchy. The boss, the chief engineer and the inspectors alike depended upon the know-how of the skilled worker, which was complementary and often superior to theirs. They had to rely on the workers' cooperation and advice, to win their respect and loyalty, whereas the skilled workers themselves needed neither the boss nor the 'officers of production' to perform work.

Thus there existed a practical and technical form of workers' power on the factory floor, a power parallel to the economic and social power of capital, capable of opposing the latter and even of contemplating its overthrow. It was not the power of *every* worker nor that of the 'collective worker'. It was the power of skilled workers who, helped and assisted by unskilled workers and labourers, stood at the top of a specifically working-class hierarchy, which was distinct from and which competed with the broader social hierarchy. There was a working-class culture, tradition and ethic with its own morality and scale of values. Those at the top of the working-class hierarchy asked nothing of the bourgeois world. Instead they were the representatives of a specific culture, able to confront their bourgeois counterparts as equals and prepared to cooperate with them in production only to the extent that the bourgeois bosses were prepared to reciprocate by recognising workers' supremacy and sovereignty in the sphere they effectively controlled.[1]

In this context, the ideas of workers' power and of revolutionary seizure of power had political connotations very different from those of the post-Taylor epoch. The working class which was then aiming to seize power was not an oppressed, ignorant, uprooted and deprived mass. It was composed of a stratum which, through its traditions, elites, culture and organisations, occupied a position of near hegemony among the mass of working people and within society as a whole. In its terms, the seizure of power did not mean replacing the bourgeoisie by installing itself at the helm of the state. Instead it meant the destruction of everything standing in the way of workers' power — notably the bourgeoisie, which lived parasitically off the exploitation of labour, and the state, whose repressive apparatus made it possible for the bourgeoisie to face popular revolts.

All these notions were implicit in the slogan, 'All factories to the workers' (*l'usine aux ouvriers*). It was the exact counterpart to an older demand: 'All land to the peasants'. In the eyes of the anarcho-syndicalist workers of the nineteenth and early twentieth centuries, there was a similarity between the land, which peasants cultivated and struggled over with a parasitical seigneurial class, and the factory, which workers 'set to work' and struggled over with a parasitical and equally idle capitalist class.

---

1. The quality and speed of German industrial development is, in large measure, the result of the relationship (subsequently termed 'paternalistic') German employers were able to establish with skilled workers. It would be worth studying the different histories of the French, British and German working-class movements from this point of view. Having been co-opted by employers from the outset, German skilled workers tended, to a greater degree than anywhere else, to take on the role of officers and junior officers of production. As a result, anarcho-syndicalism did not develop as considerably in Germany as it did in France, while mass unionism, based on unskilled workers and labourers and geared towards a more stable framework of institutional negotiation, developed sooner and more rapidly.

In retrospect, what is striking about this slogan is the light it throws upon the identification of workers with 'their' work and 'their' factory. Oppression was not as yet seen as something intrinsic to factory work itself. In theory it seemed possible then for workers to take possession of the means of production and subordinate them to *their* purposes without calling into question the nature either of what was produced or of what continued to be perceived as *their* work.

As Adriano Sofri has shown, the movement for factory councils in the early 1920s can be seen as the most advanced expression of a class of workers that felt itself able to exercise unmediated power over production and to extend this power to society as a whole.[2] Since workers were able to run the factories, they could equally run society. This was the basic premise and experience informing the concept of factory councils as the permanent organs of workers' power. It was a premise grounded upon an assumption which has subsequently disappeared. This consisted of the belief that the social process of production was as transparent and intelligible as the labour process that existed in each workshop and factory. Mastery of the latter would entail mastery of the former. Hence, the site of production was also the site of power.

None of this remains true nowadays (if it ever has been). Firstly, as we have seen, it is no longer possible to regard the factory as an economic unit. It has become a productive unit integrated with other productive units often long distances away, dependent upon a centralised management coordinating dozens of productive units for its supplies, outlets, product lines etc. In other words, the sites of production are no longer the sites of decision-making and economic power. The social process of production has become opaque, and this opacity has come to affect the work process in every technical unit. The final destination and even the very nature of what is produced remains unknown. Apart from management, nobody knows exactly what the things being produced are for — and in any event nobody gives a toss.

The same process of technical specialisation and economic

---

2. 'Sur les conseils de délégués', *Les Temps Modernes*, June 1974.

concentration that has destroyed the autonomy of the productive unit has also destroyed those trades which were the source of workers' autonomy. Instead of a hierarchy and an order in production defined by *workers*, taylorism made it possible to impose a hierarchy and order defined by the factory management. Skilled workers were eliminated after bitter conflict and replaced by 'petty officers of production' who, although of proletarian origin, formed part of the managerial hierarchy. They were chosen and trained by management and invested by it with disciplinary and police powers. Production work was henceforth carried out by an atomised mass of workers divested of autonomy and technical power.

The notion of 'taking power' over production is a meaningless one as far as this mass of workers is concerned, at least in the case of the factory *as it is*. Workers' councils — which were the organs of working-class power when production was carried out by technically autonomous teams of workers — have become anachronistic in the giant factory of assembly-lines and self-contained departments. The only imaginable form of workers' power now is the power to control and veto: the power to refuse certain conditions and types of work, to define acceptable norms and enforce respect for these norms upon the managerial hierarchy.

It is obvious, however, that this type of power is of a negative and subordinate sort. It exists *within the framework* of capitalist relations of production, *over* a labour process defined in general (if not in detail) by management. It places limits upon the power of management but does not present it with any autonomous form of workers' power. This is why, as has been the case in Italy, attempts to establish councils (at the level of the shop or line) as the expression of grass-roots workers' power, have usually resulted in their rapid re-integration into the trade-union structure and their institutionalisation as negotiating and bargaining forums.

It is difficult to see how things could be otherwise. The grass-roots workers' council has no power over the product or the process of production as a whole. What it produces is a mere component — carefully planned and predetermined by a design staff — of the whole factory's or group's output. The process of producing this component has been equally carefully planned and predetermined in the design of the special machines that have usually been pre-set in order to deprive workers of the freedom to adjust them or take initiatives. Workers or work groups are in no position to put these machines or their products to any autonomous use. Their margin of autonomy amounts to challenging the organisation and speed of the required operations, the number and length of breaks, the size of work groups and the length of the working day. These have become the variables upon which workers' demands are now centred. This is not to say that they are the most important variables in the eyes of workers; they are merely the only ones that allow some room for the expression of autonomous initiatives by work groups, the only ones that make it possible to assert *some* power.

In both France and Italy there is ample evidence that the assertion of power matters more to workers than the qualitative improvements to which it might give rise. In a typical strike in the Jaeger factories in Caen in 1972, for example, initial demands centred upon the right of working women to set themselves the speed of work. But when they were provisionally granted the right to work 'at their natural speed', they rapidly discovered that 'our natural speed is not to work at all', at least under existing social and technical conditions. The same thing happened at Fiat in Turin. When workers there were granted the right to establish councils representing each distinct work group and elect stewards (*delegati di cottimo*) in order to control those variables within their power, in many cases they continued to call into question the norms that they themselves had fixed and negotiated with management.

It is clear that once a norm has been decided upon by workers and accepted by management, it becomes no more than a new form of imprisonment for the workers themselves. It matters little whether it is any the more bearable physically or psychologically. Once it has been recognised and ratified by management it no longer expresses the autonomous power of the work group but reflects the constricting power of the managerial hierarchy. In any event, the latter cannot grant any real power to work groups, even over the variables they control. Factories can only work if the outputs of the various lines, workshops and teams are coordinated and regular. Although buffer stocks may allow some flexibility in the speed of work, they do not make for complete elasticity. This is why management (whatever the type of ownership of a factory) in exchange for granting the right to self-determination, expects work groups to adhere to the norms they might define.

In this situation, the *delegati di cottimo* or shop stewards are bound to find themselves in a highly uncomfortable position. Originally elected by ordinary workers, they are mandated to impose the latter's demands upon management. But as soon as they succeed in having their demands accepted by management, these demands become a commitment of the work group to adhere to the norms which it has itself defined, and the stewards become responsible to management for ensuring that the undertaking will be respected. Hence the stewards, in the workers' eyes (and in their own), are transformed into representatives of management. If they refuse the role of enjoining workers 'to respect their undertakings', they will no longer be recognised by management as representatives of the grass roots; they will be unable to go back to negotiate on future occasions. There will be no other way open to them than to resign. This indeed is what the majority of those elected to represent 'workers' autonomy' chose to do. Those who did not resign became ordinary trade-union officials mediating institutionally between grass-roots aspirations and the overriding imperatives of the productive machine (imperatives represented, but not invented, by management).

Grass-roots workers' power can thus be seen to be a material impossibility within the framework of the existing structure of production. All that is actually possible is the power of trade unions, that is the power of the institutional apparatus to which workers delegate representative power. Trade-union power is not, however, the same thing as workers' power, any more than the power of parliament is the power of the sovereign people. Unions possess power *as institutions* that are relatively autonomous from their mandators. They become autonomous as a result of the mediatory power conferred upon them by their institutional role. There is no point in reproving individual trade unionists for this fact. They sometimes experience the contradiction as a source of anguish or misery. Not they individually are at fault but the technical and social division of labour, the mode and relations of production, the size and inertia of the industrial machine which, because they rigidly predetermine both the results and the phases of the work process, leave no more than marginal space for workers' control in and over production.

If workers' control is to exist, it is therefore necessary to go about enlarging this space. This is hardly a small matter. For the obstacle standing in the way of workers' control, power and autonomy is not merely legal or institutional. It is also a material obstacle, which derives from the design, size and functioning of factories. It ultimately derives from the 'collective capitalist' responsible for the management of all factories. For the great secret of large-scale industry, as of any vast bureaucratic or military machine, is that *nobody holds power*. Power in such organisms does not have a subject; it is not the property of individuals freely defining the rules and goals of their collective actions. Instead, all that can be found — from the bottom right up to the top of an industrial or administrative hierarchy — are agents obeying the categorical imperatives and inertias of the material system they serve. The personal power of capitalists, directors and managers of every kind is an optical illusion. It is a power that exists only in the eyes of those lower down the hierarchy who receive orders from 'those above' and are personally at their mercy.

In fact 'those above' are not the sovereign authors of the orders they give; they too are no more than mere agents. There is a higher law for whose formulation no one in particular is responsible, which they are bound to obey or go to their doom. Its terms consist of injunctions like 'capital must grow'; 'orders must come in'; 'competitors must be eliminated'; 'machines must be kept working'. More, quicker, bigger, cheaper... these are the laws of capital.

Marx described capitalists as functionaries of capital: at once oppressors and alienated, they have to submit to and uphold what appears to be a law beyond their power. They administer the workings of capital; they do not control them. They do not possess power; rather, they are possessed by it. Power is not a subject. It is a system of relationships, a structure. It is managed, not owned by the collective capitalist. And this fact, this infinite dilution of power within the order of things, endows those who are its agents with their legitimacy. Thus at any moment, anyone of them may say, 'I'm not doing this because I want to but because

I have to. I am not carrying out my free will but submitting to the iron law of necessity. I don't make the rules, I just obey them like all of us. If you know of any other way to run this firm, tell me and you can have my place.'

All modern forms of power are of this type. They have no subject. They are not borne or assumed by any sovereign claiming to be the source of all law and the basis of all legitimacy. In the modern state, there are no rulers enforcing obedience by virtue of command, or requiring allegiance and submission to their person. In the modern state, the bearers of power enforce obedience in the name of objective necessities for which no one can be held responsible. Contemporary technocratic power has an essentially *functional* legitimacy. It does not belong to an individual subject but to a function, to the place occupied by an individual within the organigramme of a firm, an institution or the state. The particular individuals holding this or that functional position are always contingent, can always be called into question. They have no majesty or moral authority. Malicious gossips circulate on their account; people laugh behind their backs since *as individuals* the holders of public positions are no better than anyone else — and can be replaced from one day to the next. Power neither belongs to them nor emanates from them. *It is an effect of the system*. It is the result of the structure of a material system of relationships in which a law appearing to govern things subjugates people through the mediation of other people.

It matters little here whether this type of material system was established deliberately to create this sort of subjugation. What is important is that the latter cannot be abolished without the abolition of the former. The industrial system as we know it results in subjugation to the giant technical and bureaucratic machines and in the power of capital through the mediation of its functionaries. Eliminating the latter without eliminating the former in its totality would amount to no more than the substitution of one bourgeoisie for another.

5. Personal Power and Functional Power

The working-class movement has known from its early beginnings that there is a difference between personal and functional power. The former reflects a person's superior capacity and knowledge, whatever her or his hierarchical position. A skilled worker, for instance, can direct unskilled labourers because of superior know-how, and feels entitled to the acknowledgement of this superiority: anarcho-syndicalism went hand in hand with a corporatist mentality and a sense of trade-based elitism.

On the other hand, anarcho-syndicalist workers challenged the power of their bosses, which was derived not from superior know-how, but merely from the dominant position conferred by law and the framework of social relations upon the legal owners of capital. Any fool could become a boss by inheriting a business, a fortune and the name or title to which legal rights, a social position and a place within the institutional hierarchy were attached.

While fighting the capitalist bosses as a class and as a function, anarcho-syndicalists did not refuse to reach an understanding with certain 'Schumpeterian' entrepreneurs, typified by the 'self-made man' with a passion for technical prowess and appreciation of work well done. The personal power of this type of entrepreneur was, to a large extent, based upon ability to convince his workers of his superior technical competence within his own field, and hence to create a sense of shared commitment among all those who had capability and a willingness to make the enterprise a success. Class antagonism has often been superseded by this type of relationship between skilled workers and the personal power of visionary entrepreneurs. It is because they were passionately personal that the goals of the 'Schumpeterian entrepreneur' could transcend class barriers and be accepted or even shared by the workers.

The worst form of power is not, then, the personal power of a leader or a head imposing sovereign will upon others and expecting them to pursue aims which the leader alone has freely chosen. This type of personal power implies a certain sort of risk. By setting forth a specifically personal project and by taking full responsibility for her or his actions, self-made entrepreneurs necessarily run the risk of being challenged. They are likely to be admired or detested according to their success or failure in getting those over whom they have authority to share their goals. They work without legal protection or even legitimacy. Saying 'I want' makes it impossible for them to take refuge behind overriding external necessity or impersonal forces. Since the entrepreneur's power is that of a subject-person, it can be opposed, called into question, even rejected by those under command. The exercise of personal power necessarily implies an acceptance of the most direct, personal forms of conflict. The act of asserting one's own will carries the risk that others will respond by asserting theirs.

Consequently, Schumpeterian types of entrepreneur and visionary industrial 'pioneers' tend to live in an atmosphere of passion and drama. Their relationships with their immediate entourage are often intensely emotional. All the parties involved are aware that they may meet total defeat. Although obviously class relations, none of those involved in them behaves entirely in accordance with the legal and institutional rules informing the relationship. The personal power of the boss may be destroyed, bringing down the whole enterprise. Doubtless other enterprises will take its place in which the power of capital rests upon a less fragile basis than the personal authority of an entrepreneur. But what sort of basis might this be?

The foundation of the legitimacy of power is one of the great unresolved questions of capitalist society. According to its own ideology, the most able should always have unrestricted access to the positions of power. Liberal ideology implies a meritocracy and this, in its turn — since individual capacities and abilities are by nature untransmissible and personal — presupposes complete fluidity in relation to power. No material or institutional inertia must frustrate social mobility. Yesterday's winner must be liable to be displaced today by whoever shows greater ability. Employers and workers, bankers and peasants must be able to permute their respective social positions constantly. Liberal ideology assumes that success in business never provides the victors with the means to preserve their own power. If free enterprise and competition are to prevail, the power derived from success in business must not imply the power to block the ascent to newcomers and to transmit to heirs or delegate to trustees the prerogatives and privileges one has won.

This ideal vision of a society of free and equal citizens might have contained a germ of truth during the heroic age of capitalism, which was also the age of the colonisation of North America. It presupposed practically unlimited opportunities for enterprise and success and implied that no one would be barred from succeeding by those who were successful before. Stating this presupposition makes it obvious that it could only come true in exceptional circumstances and for a limited duration. There are only so many positions of power at any moment in any given society. Further, and despite the implicit assumptions of liberal ideology, there are no forms of power which are not, in essence, also the power to secure and delegate. Power, by definition, is an appropriation of a position of domination, and such positions are necessarily privileged and scarce. Any occupant of such a position necessarily denies it to others. It follows that the only politically important question is this: was the position of domination *created* by its occupant and is the power which it confers destined to disappear along with the individual? Or, on the other hand, is power inherent in the *pre-existing position* occupied by its holder within a system of social relations and is it, as a result, independent of the individual occupying it?

As a society ages — and this is particularly true of capitalist society — positions of power and the modalities by which they are exercised tend to become increasingly (and in the last analysis, completely) predetermined. Every position, and all the personal qualities associated with it, come to be predefined. Hence no one, however audacious, will be allowed to succeed outside the customary channels or the established institutions. Power will never be exercised by individuals or depend exclusively upon their personal authority. It comes to be exercised through institutions, following predetermined procedures, and those responsible for its exercise are themselves no more than the servants of an apparatus of domination ('a machine' as the

Americans put it, or 'the establishment' as it is known in Britain). They impersonate an impersonal and transcendent power.

This institutional sclerosis is inseparable from the bureaucratisation of power. No one is allowed to conquer power by and for her or himself. All she or he can do is to rise to one of the positions conferring a modicum of power on its holders. Consequently, it's no longer people who have power; it's the positions of power which have their people. These positions are no longer tailored by powerful individualities to fit and exalt their ego. Instead they tailor the individuals to make them fit their function. Such a society leaves no room for adventurers, Schumpeterian entrepreneurs or conquerors. Success belongs to careerists, to those who have followed the paths and attended the schools that equip them with the personality, accent, manners and social skills fitting the functions that look for people to fill them.

This development was already pre-ordained from the moment when the individual capitalist gave way to the joint stock company, the entrepreneur to the bank and the boss to capital and its functionaries — otherwise known as managers. The whole machinery of economic and political decision-making and management has come to be structured in a way that meets the requirements of the profitability and circulation of capital. The logic of capital must no longer be dependent upon the personal skills and initiatives of its servants. It must prevail whatever the abilities and individual authority of its functionaries. Naturally, the same situation is true of the mechanisms of political power. They are called upon to exercise power over people without allowing anyone in particular to exercise it in any personal sense. The state might be defined as a mechanism of power to which every citizen is subordinated and which, at the same time, denies personal power to everyone.

This type of society finds its fullest expression in the figure of the bureaucrat. Bureaucrats guarantee the power of the state without possessing any power themselves. As agents of power or fragments of power, they maintain the mechanisms of domination by enforcing rules for which they have no responsibility and by fulfilling functions with which they can have no personal identification. The power of bureaucrats varies inversely with their impotence; they uphold the integrity of the administrative machine by renouncing all power for themselves. They are the cogs of a well-defined machine, the instruments of a power exercised without a subjective will behind it. In the state apparatus as in the giant firm, power is an organigramme.

It has been rightly said that the organigramme was invented in order to produce more or less automatic obedience to the imperatives of the hierarchy. It was conceived by those technicians of power known as operational researchers (or occasionally by lawyers). Its object is to pre-ordain the working of a system by breaking it down into narrowly specialised functions and predefining the points of lateral and vertical junction between the specialised tasks. A network of functions, checks and coordinations regulates the circulation of fragmentary information and decisions, defines limited powers designed to balance and exclude one another in such a way as to prevent any individual or group from occupying a position of supremacy. Although an organigramme may be the creation of a single individual, this does not mean that it can be seen as the materialisation of that individual's power. A management consultant or specialist of constitutional law has no more personal power than any other functionary; they merely specialise in devising forms of domination over everyone, implemented through the non-power of each.

The elimination of personal power to the benefit of the functional power inherent in an anonymous organigramme has profoundly changed the implications of class conflict. Power in both society and the firm is now *exercised* by people who do not *hold* it, who are not personally answerable for their actions and take refuge behind the functions which answer for them. Since they are executants or servants, bureaucrats are never responsible. The predefined obligations inherent in their function relieve them of all personal responsibility and decision and enable them to meet protest with the disarming reply: 'We haven't chosen to do this. We're only enforcing the regulations. We're carrying out orders.' Whose orders? Whose regulations? One could go back indefinitely up the hierarchy and it would still be impossible to find anyone else to say, 'Mine'. However obvious the class character of the system of domination, it does not follow that the individuals making up the dominant class are exercising domination individually. They too are dominated by the very power they exercise. The subject of this power is untraceable, which is why the dominated masses tend implicitly to call for a sovereign whom they could hold responsible and to whom they could present their demands or appeals. Think of the slogans of mass demonstrations and the litany of chants directed at named individuals: de Gaulle or Giscard, Wilson or Thatcher (e.g. 'the milk-snatcher').

The trap is obvious. Ascribing the effects of a system to a supposed sovereign, held personally responsible for its shortcomings, leads to expecting salvation from a real leader willing to take personal responsibility for making matters change. This type of appeal to a prestigious figurehead (or 'saviour') against the effects of bureaucratic domination is not limited to the petty bourgeoisie. When an oppressed mass finds itself without the practical or theoretical means to fight an illegitimate system of domination, recourse to the personal power of a prestigious leader may seem a desirable course to follow. By the mere fact of announcing: 'This is my decision; this is my will; these are my orders', the leader may deliver the people from the glue of serial impotence. In contradistinction to a system based upon the evasion of responsibility, anonymous bureaucracies and impotent petty tyrants exercising a nameless power and complaining endlessly that they don't do what they want and do not want what they are doing, a leader or Führer is first and foremost that 'grand individual' willing to say, 'I'. Power, all power, is with this leader who will answer personally for his or her doings. The leader will be the solace and salvation of all those vainly seeking to bring to account the people responsible for their humiliations. He or she will identify and indict the culprits: it's pusillanimous and selfish petty bourgeois; it's 'plutocrats' and sinister 'cosmopolitans' who, behind the scenes, weave their occult web of price-fixing, bribery and secret international manoeuvre; it's the corrupt and discredited politicians willing to prostitute themselves to a ruling class only too willing to set its blighted interests above those of the nation. The rhetoric is familiar. People awake, heed the call of the Führer whose grand design will sweep away the miserable projects of the bourgeoisie; who will free you from an oppressive system created by no one, for whose existence no one takes responsibility; who will impose personal power upon history and replace the mysterious laws governing

the order of things by fiat. Henceforth everything that is done
will be done by the Führer's will: 'Lead, Führer, we will follow'
— and recover our humanity and grandeur through the act of
obedience.

Such is the language of fascism. It has a capacity to transcend
class division and draw upon the frustrated needs generated by a
system of impersonal domination based upon the impotence of
each and all. An indispensable condition for the emergence of
fascism is the existence of a leader with a mass following, both
prestigious and plebeian, capable of embodying the majesty of
the state and the individuality of the 'common' person, endowed
with unlimited power.[1] In the absence of this type of charismatic
leader the totalitarian state may take the shape of military dictatorship, plebiscitary monarchy or police state, but not of
fascism.

Fascism is specific in its way of enabling the people to identify
with the all-powerful leader. The Führer exercises by proxy the
power that belongs to anyone; he stands for the ordinary person,
strong and courageous enough to drive away all those profiteers,
exploiters, parasites, bureaucrats and politicians who are
enmeshing the people within an anonymous system and depriv-
ing it of its will. Fascism implies the abolition of functional
power at every level and its replacement by the personal power
of the strongest and most able. It puts an end to 'the system'.
Henceforth all power shall reflect the superior abilities of those
in command. Only 'the best' will stand at the head of society and
the party. The quality of individuals will become the basis of
hierarchy within society and the mass organisations (of youth,
women, workers, trades-guilds, etc.). Promotion by means of
'connections' and protections will be made impossible, and
therefore occult networks of freemasons, Jews or bourgeois
associations will be eradicated. The old 'decadent', 'degenerate',
and 'corrupt' elite consisted of a mafia who monopolises the
best positions without, of course, being in any way 'the best' —

---

1. The circumstances allowing for the emergence of this type of leader are
necessarily exceptional. Only their absence explains the weakness of fascism in
France. Pétain and de Gaulle were prestigious figures but had no mass following.
Doriot and Poujade had the qualities of plebeian leaders but had no prestige or
sense of the majesty of the state.

except at the sordid art of intrigue.

A new plebeian elite will sweep away all this rot. It will ensure an identity between the hierarchy of functions and of capabilities. Fascism goes to great lengths (particularly through decorations, insignia and uniforms) in the establishment of all sorts of hierarchies between people. Sports competitions, games and tournaments play a substantial role in the selection of the 'most able'. Physical prowess is a cardinal value since the physical superiority of the stronger over the weaker is, of all types of superiority, the least questionable, most easily measurable and most obviously ontological. Holders of muscular strength and physical dexterity *are* powerful by themselves. The power they draw from their strength owes nothing to social position, connections or cultural mediation. Fascism is a virile cultural revolution. It aims at liquidating bourgeois values (property, saving, culture, family life, privacy, good manners, charity, tolerance etc.), and substituting the so-called vital values.[2] It expects its leaders to excel in these (at least in appearance). Hence its frequent borrowings from feudal society. Fascism aims to be a brutal and barbaric liberation, the unshackling of the power of those whose strength has hitherto been held in check by the furtive manoeuvres of profiteers. In place of the old state, whose machinery of domination was dominated by nobody and where no one had power over the structure of power, the new state will be a pyramid of personal powers impelled by one and the same common will, that of 'our beloved leader'.

This at any rate is the ideology of fascism. It rejects political parties and 'the party system' not simply, as has often been said, because it is based on the will of and permanent unmediated, communion between the Führer and the people; but more fundamentally because fascism replaces an anonymous system of power with the power of a person. The specific aim of political parties is to seek to place their members in the control room of the state machinery. All parties are alike in this respect. They are all replicas of the state apparatus which they seek to control.

---

2. I have developed these themes in *Fondements pour une morale*, Paris, Galilée 1977.

They are all associations of people aspiring to some sort of functional power, prepared to share out key government posts among themselves by a combination of intrigue, negotiation, wheeling and dealing, betrayal and blackmail. Once there, following the laws of the system, they will only display their personal impotence. For fascism, the abolition of parties is inherent in the abolition of the aimless machinery of impersonal power which is the state.

This is a long way from the simplistic explanation of fascism as a device invented by monopoly capital to serve as a diversion from economic crisis, drawing its support from a reactionary middle class threatened with proletarianisation. In fact fascist ideology is an expression and mobilisation of a set of needs, frustrations and aspirations created by the system of domination specific to industrialised societies. The themes of fascist ideology can be found permanently, if in diffused form, among all levels and classes of society, especially among the popular classes (and, in France, in the speeches of the Communist Party leadership). But only in exceptional circumstances (such as an economic crisis blocking social mobility) and with a charismatic leadership can these themes and the masses who spontaneously propagate them give rise to a radicalised political movement.

The replacement of a system of functional domination by the continuous promotion of the most able; the replacement of a class monopolising positions of power by the personal power of a Führer; and the elimination of the state and its bureaucracy in favour of mass organisations mobilised by a single will and goal — all this amounts to a radical transformation of society and the state and a complete overhaul of every existing institution. In some respects it is an agenda resembling that of the socialist movement. Yet all of these transformations also imply transformations in the productive system, the elimination of the giant technical machineries, administrative and economic units — in short, of every institutional agency whose size and complexity are not susceptible to control by personal power and which therefore require a functional division of tasks, including those of management. Nothing of the sort has ever been envisaged by fascism. Instead the Führer principle — according to which everything, at every level, is subject to the personal will and power of the Führer — requires increased centralisation within the machinery of domination in order to ensure that no personal power can be exercised outside that of the Führer. The machinery of power must therefore be cast in the mould of a military machine, with its ranks, hierarchical controls, rules of obedience and strict discipline. The only power permitted outside that of the Führer is the power delegated to revocable underlings acting 'in the Führer's name'. Thus instead of the promotion of the most able, lower leadership tends to be selected on the basis of loyalty and reliability. Competitive conformism and servility towards the 'beloved leader' and the leader's representatives tend to become the major qualities required of those seeking to make a career.

Thus the personal power of the Führer functions as a sort of ideological cover for the total bureaucratisation of public life. Consequently fascist states tend to present the worst failings and perversions of the bureaucratic capitalist state in exaggerated form. Moreover, it is no longer possible to point them out. Official propaganda insists upon their disappearance and there are no means of opposing the official line. The Führer and entourage are presented as the heroes of the historical epic in progress and the authors of every decision that has been taken. The implementation of decisions requires the militarisation of both economic and administrative activities with all its ensuing waste, corruption, nepotism, black marketeering and unaccountability. Hitler's and Stalin's police states were remarkably similar in this respect. Thus in modern societies, the abolition of functional in favour of personal power finally results in dictatorship by the holders of functional power and personification of the machinery of domination.

This digression should help us to situate the problem of power more precisely. In modern societies, power does not have a subject. It only appears to be personal. In reality it is the effect of a structure; it derives from the existence of a machinery of domination which endows with functional powers those holding positions within it, whatever the nature of their abilities or political options. As long as this machinery of domination remains intact, it is politically immaterial who the holders of positions of power may be. It is the structure of the machinery which will determine the nature of power and mode of government, the relationship between civil society and the political

society and between the political society and the state. The belief
that the machinery of domination needs to be taken over in
order to subsequently change it has been a long-standing illusion
of reformists. This is not to say that reformism has not carried
out reforms. It has however failed to change either the nature of
power, the mode of government or the relationship between civil
society and the state. Its reforms have only served to reinforce
and legitimate the machinery of power, the domination over the
masses and their impotence.

By its nature the proletariat is incapable of becoming the subject of power. If its representatives take over the machinery of
domination deployed by capital, they will succeed only in producing the very same type of domination and, in their turn,
become a functional bourgeoisie. A class cannot overthrow
another class merely by taking its place within the system of
domination. All it will thereby achieve will be a permutation of
office-holders and by no means a transfer of power. The notion
that the domination of capital can be transferred to the proletariat and thereby 'collectivised' is as farcical as the ideal of
making nuclear power stations 'democratic' by transferring their
management to the control of the trade-union hierarchies.

The concept of seizure of power needs to be fundamentally
revised. Power can only be seized by an already *existing* dominant
class. Taking power implies taking it away from its holders, not
by occupying their posts but by making it permanently
impossible for them to keep their machinery of domination running. Revolution is first and foremost the irreversible destruction of this machinery. It implies a form of collective practice
capable of bypassing and superseding it through the development of an alternative network of relations. The day a new
machinery of domination conferring functional powers on the
rulers is generated by these practices, the revolution will have
come to an end. A new institutional order will have been
established.

Previous revolutions have generally sought to eliminate all
types of functional power so as to do away with all forms of
domination. They have generally failed. Functional power has
inevitably arisen anew from the machineries of social production
and the division of labour underpinning them. We therefore
cannot expect to eliminate relations of domination as a result of

eliminating functional power. The only hope of abolishing relations of domination is to start by recognising that functional power is inevitable. This recognition will enable us to look for ways of effectively restricting it to areas where it cannot be dispensed with. This will teach us to dissociate power from domination, keeping the first where necessary, doing away with the latter everywhere and upholding the specific autonomies of civil society, the political society and the state.

6. A New Historical Subject:
The Non-Class of Post-Industrial Proletarians

The crisis of socialism is above all a reflection of the crisis of the proletariat. The disappearance of the polyvalent skilled worker — the possible subject of productive labour and hence of a revolutionary transformation of social relations — has also entailed the disappearance of the class able to take charge of the socialist project and translate it into reality. Fundamentally, the degeneration of socialist theory and practice has its origins here.

In Marx 'scientific socialism' rested on a dual foundation. Firstly, it was a project carried by a class of proletarianised social producers that formed a virtual majority of the population. Secondly, this class was defined, in essence, by conscious rejection of its class being. Each proletarian, as a member of the class, was a living contradiction between his or her sovereign productive praxis and the commodity status which capitalist social relations conferred upon it by reducing it to an undifferentiated quantum of exploited labour. The proletariat was the potential subject of socialist revolution because each proletarian experienced a contradiction between sovereignty over her or his work and work relationships, and the negation of this sovereignty by capital. Class unity and class consciousness were based upon the inevitability that each proletarian would, in his or her own activity, encounter the general negation of the sovereignty of all proletarian.

Class being was the intolerable and ubiquitous external limit to the activity of each and every class member. The proletariat was the only class, and the first in history, which had no interest but to cancel its class being by destroying the external constraints by which it had been constituted. For Marx, then, the proletariat was itself the negation of its own being. The task of 'scientific socialism' was merely to demonstrate how this negation could become operationally effective and pass into positivity.

As we have seen, however, the capitalist division of labour has destroyed the dual premise of 'scientific socialism'. In the first place, the worker's labour no longer involves any power. A class whose social activity yields no power does not have the means to take power, nor does it feel called upon to do so. In the second place, work is no longer the worker's own activity. In the immense majority of cases, whether in the factory or the office, work is now a passive, pre-programmed activity which has been totally subordinated to the working of a big machinery, leaving no room for personal initiative. It is no longer possible for workers to identify with 'their' work or 'their' function in the productive process. Everything now appears to take place outside themselves. 'Work' itself has become a quantum of reified activity awaiting and subjugating the 'worker'.

Loss of the ability to identify with one's work is tantamount to the disappearance of any sense of belonging to a class. Just as work remains external to the individual, so too does class being. Just as work has become a nondescript task carried out without any personal involvement, which one may quit for another, equally contingent job, so too has class membership come to be lived as a contingent and meaningless fact.

For workers, it is no longer a question of freeing themselves *within* work, putting themselves in control of work, or seizing power within the framework of their work. The point now is to free oneself *from* work by rejecting its nature, content, necessity and modalities. But to reject work is also to reject the traditional strategy and organisational forms of the working-class movement. It is no longer a question of winning power as a worker, but of winning the power no longer to function as a worker. The power at issue is not at all the same as before. The class itself has entered into crisis.

This crisis, however, is much more a crisis of a myth and an ideology than of a really existing working class. For over a century the idea of the proletariat has succeeded in masking its own unreality. This idea is now as obsolete as the proletariat itself, since in place of the productive collective worker of old, a nonclass of non-workers is coming into being, prefiguring a nonsociety within existing society in which classes will be abolished along with work itself and all forms of domination.

In contradistinction to the working class, this non-class has not been engendered by capitalism and marked with the insignia of capitalist relations of production. It is the result of the crisis of capitalism and the dissolution of the social relations of capitalist production — a process stemming from the growth of new production technology. The negativity which, according to Marx, was to be embodied in the working class has by no means disappeared. It has been displaced and has acquired a more radical form in a new social area. As it has shifted, it has acquired a new form and content which directly negate the ideology, the material base, the social relations and the juridical organisation (or state form) of capitalism. It has the added advantage over Marx's working class of being immediately conscious of itself; its existence is at once indissolubly subjective and objective, collective and individual.

This non-class emcompasses all those who have been expelled from production by the abolition of work, or whose capacities are under-employed as a result of the industrialisation (in this case, the automation and computerisation) of intellectual work. It includes all the supernumeraries of present-day social production, who are potentially or actually unemployed, whether permanently or temporarily, partially or completely. It results from the decomposition of the old society based upon the dignity, value, social utility and desirability of work. It stretches into virtually every layer of society, well beyond those 'lumpen' whom the Black Panthers, with remarkable prescience, counterposed in the late 1960s to the class of unionised, stably employed workers, protected by labour legislation and collective agreements.[1]

---

1. The Black Panthers gave the word 'lumpen' a very much wider meaning than it has in German and in Marx's definition of the 'lumpenproletariat' (literally, proletariat in rags). They defined the traditional, stable, unionised working class, whose position was protected by collective agreements, as a minority of privileged reactionaries, a vestige of the industrial economy.

The notion of a post-industrial economy and proletariat was widely adopted among marxist revolutionaries in North and South America in the late 1960s. One of the most remarkable theorists of that period, Ladislas Dowbor, alias Jamil, one of the founders of the VPR (Vanguardia Popular Revolucionaria) of Brazil states:

That traditional working class is now no more than a privileged minority. The majority of the population now belong to the post-industrial neo-proletariat which, with no job security or definite class identity, fills the area of probationary, contracted, casual, temporary and part-time employment. In the not too distant future, jobs such as these will be largely eliminated by automation. Even now, their specifications are continually changing with the rapid development of technology, and their requirements bear little relation to the knowledge and skills offered by schools and universities. The neo-proletariat is generally over-qualified for the jobs it finds. It is generally condemned

---

> In the modern sector [of the Brazilian economy] there are factories in which so large an amount of capital has been tied up that it would be counter-productive not to pay the workers a decent wage. But the number of workers needed is shrinking and the share of wages in production costs is declining. So a decent wage is being paid to an ever smaller number of workers.
>
> The growth of the modernised sector generates the crisis of traditional industries... They are obliged either to modernise in their turn, or to disappear. As a result, the working class is progressively expelled from the process of production, swelling the class of marginals and leaving an ever smaller, better paid and relatively satisfied working class which has no inclination at all towards the revolution.

Like the Black Panthers and, subsequently, certain components of the 'autonomous' left in Italy, the VPR believed in the revolutionary inclination of the 'marginal classes', who:

> live in permanently violent conditions as a result of police harassment, the usurpation of their land, the loss of their jobs and the condition of illegality in which they are forced to live when they flock to the towns. This mass of people is extremely responsive to our type of action: armed, violent action. (From an interview given to Sanche Gramont in *The New York Times*, 15 November 1970)

In fact, contrary to theories in vogue at the time, armed violent action has never led to a 'people's war' in any country. It has led to counter-guerilla campaigns which have usually been able to liquidate both supporters and sympathisers of armed struggle, together with all forms of political opposition to repression. When the police turn to the same form of clandestine terrorist organisation as their revolutionary counterparts, they have usually been able to annihilate them without much difficulty — once all legal and juridical barriers to police terrorism have been waived. Even in traditionally democratic states like Uruguay, armed action has led to the suppression of a legal system whose existence initially allowed such struggles to develop.

to under-use of its capacities when it is in work, and to unemployment itself in the longer term. Any employment seems to be accidental and provisional, every type of work purely contingent. It cannot feel any involvement with 'its' work or identification with 'its' job. Work no longer signifies an activity or even a major occupation; it is merely a blank interval on the margins of life, to be endured in order to earn a little money.[2]

In contrast to the proletariat in Marx's theory,[3] the neo-proletariat does not define itself by reference to 'its' work and cannot be defined in terms of its position within the social process of production. The question of who does or does not belong to the class of productive workers — how to categorise a kinesitherapist, a tourist guide, an airline employee, a systems analyst, a technician in a biological laboratory or a telecommunications engineer has no meaning or importance when set against a growing and more or less numerically dominant mass of people moving from one 'job' to another. Learning trades they will never regularly practise, following courses without outlets or practical utility, giving them up or failing them because 'after all, what does it matter', they go on to work in the post office during the summer, to pick grapes in the autumn, to join a department-store staff for Christmas, and to work as a labourer in the spring...

The only certainty, as far as they are concerned, is that they do not feel they belong to the working class, *or to any other class*. They do not recognise themselves in the term 'worker' or in its symmetrical opposite, 'unemployed'. Whether they work in a bank, the civil service, a cleaning agency or a factory, neo-proletarians are basically non-workers temporarily doing

---

2. The practice of 'job-sharing', which has become more and more widespread in the United States and the Scandinavian countries, is of some significance in this context.

3. However, Marx was very well aware that the socialisation of production would lead to 'indifference towards any specific kind of labour', corresponding

to a form of society in which individuals can with ease transfer from one labour to another, and where the specific kind is a matter of chance for them, hence of indifference. Labour... has ceased to be organically linked with particular individuals in any specific form.

Grundrisse, Harmondsworth, Penguin 1973, p.104.

something that means nothing to them. They do 'any old thing' which 'anyone' could do, provisionally engaged in temporary and nameless work. For them work is no longer an individual contribution to the total production of society made up of countless individual activities. Social production is now given first, and work is merely the mass of insecure, short-term activities to which it gives rise. Workers no longer 'produce' society through the mediation of the relations of production; instead, the machinery of social production as a whole produces 'work' and imposes it in a random way upon random, interchangeable individuals. Work, in other words, does not belong to the individuals who perform it, nor can it be termed their own activity. It belongs to the machinery of social production, is allocated and programmed by it, remaining external to the individuals upon whom it is imposed. Instead of being the worker's mode of insertion into a system of universal cooperation, work is now the mode of subordination to the machinery of universal domination. Instead of generating workers able to transcend their finite particularity and define themselves directly as social producers in general, work has come to be perceived by individuals as the contingent form of social oppression in general. The proletariat which the young Marx saw as a universal force void of any particularised form has become a particularised individuality in revolt against the universal force of the apparatus.[4]

The inversion of the marxist concept of the proletariat is thus total. Not only does the new post-industrial proletariat not find

---

4. After describing with remarkable prescience the separation of the labourer from science and technology, as they acquired the reified form of fixed capital in the means of production, Marx went on nevertheless to predict that, thanks to the freeing of time, fully developed individuals would become the subjects and agents of the immediate process of production:

> This process is then both discipline, as regards the human being in the process of becoming; and, at the same time, practice (*Ausübung*), experimental science, materially creative and objectifying science, as regards the human being who has become, *in whose head exists the accumulated knowledge of society.*
> (*Grundrisse, op. cit.* p. 712 (my italics))

The polytechnic and scientific development of the individual through automation is an illusion shared by Marx and the 'modernists' of Eastern Europe in the 1960s.

any source of potential power in socialised labour: all it finds there is the reality of apparatus power and its own impotence. Not only is it no longer the possible subjective agent of socialised productive labour: instead, it defines its own subjectivity through the refusal of socialised labour and the negation of work perceived itself as a negation (or alienation). Nothing indicates that this total alienation of socialised work can be reversed. Technological development does not point towards a possible appropriation of social production by the producers. Instead it indicates further elimination of the social producer, and continuing marginalisation of socially necessary labour as a result of the computer revolution.[5] Whatever the number of jobs remaining in industry and the service sector once automation has been fully achieved, they will be incapable of providing identity, meaning and power for those who fill them. For there is a rapid decline in the amount of labour-time necessary to reproduce not *this* society and its mechanisms of domination and command, but a viable society endowed with everything useful and necessary to life. The requirement could be a mere two hours a day, or ten hours a week, or fifteen weeks a year, or ten years in a lifetime.

The substantially longer period of social labour maintained in contemporary society has accelerated rather than slowed down the devaluation, in the ethical sense, of all forms of work. The amount of time spent working and the relatively high level of employment have been artificially maintained because of the inextricable confusion which exists between the production of the necessary and the superfluous, the useful and the useless, waste and wealth, pleasures and nuisances, destruction and repair. Whole areas of economic life now have the sole function of 'providing work', or of producing for the sake of keeping people working. But when a society produces in order to provide work rather than works in order to produce, then work as a whole has no meaning. Its chief objective is simply 'to keep people occupied', and thereby to preserve the relations of subordination, competition and discipline upon which the workings of the dominant system are based.[6] Work in general comes to be

---

5. See Appendix I below.
6. *ibid*.

tainted with the suspicion that it is but a useless compulsion devised to mask the fact of each individual's redundancy or, to put it another way, to conceal *the possibility of liberation from socialised labour itself* and the obsolescence of a system of social relations which makes socialised labour the precondition of both income and the circulation of wealth.

The specificity of the post-industrial proletariat follows from this analysis. In contradistinction to the traditional working class, this non-class is free subjectivity. While the industrial proletariat derived an objective power from the transformation of matter, so that it perceived itself as a material force underpinning the whole course of society, the neo-proletariat can be defined as a non-force, without objective social importance, excluded from society. Since it plays no part in the production of society, it envisages society's development as something external, akin to a spectacle or a show. It sees no point in taking over the machine-like structure which, as it sees it, defines contemporary society, nor of placing anything whatsoever under its control. What matters instead is to appropriate areas of autonomy outside of, and in opposition to, the logic of society, so as to allow the unobstructed realisation of individual development *alongside* and *over* that machine-like structure.

The lack of an overall conception of future society fundamentally distinguishes the new post-industrial proletariat from the class which, according to Marx, was invested with a historical mission. The neo-proletariat has nothing to expect *of* contemporary society nor of its subsequent evolution. That process — the development of the productive forces — has reached its end by making work virtually superfluous. It can go no further. The logic of capital, which, after two centuries of 'progress', has led to this outcome through the accumulation of ever more efficient means of production, can offer no more and no better. More precisely, productivist industrial society can only continue by offering more and worse — more destruction, more waste, more repairs to destruction, more programming of the most intimate facets of individual life. 'Progress' has arrived at a threshold beyond which plus turns into minus. The future is heavy with menace and devoid of promise. The forward march of productivism now brings the advance of barbarism and oppression.

There is therefore no point in wondering where we are going

or in seeking to identify with laws immanent in historical development. We are not going anywhere: History has no meaning. There is nothing to be hoped from history, and no reason to sacrifice anything to that idol. No longer can we give ourselves to a transcendent cause, expecting that it will repay our suffering and reward our sacrifice with interest. We must, however, be clear about what we desire. The logic of capital has brought us to the threshold of liberation. But it can only be crossed at the price of a radical break, in which productivism is replaced by a different rationality. This rupture can only come from individuals themselves. The realm of freedom can never arise out of material processes; it can only be established by a constitutive act which, aware of its free subjectivity, asserts itself as an absolute end in itself within each individual. Only the non-class of non-producers is capable of such an act. For it alone embodies what lies beyond productivism: the rejection of the accumulation ethic and the dissolution of all classes.

7. The Post-Industrial Revolution

Both the strength and the weakness of the post-industrial proletariat lie in the fact that it does not have an overall vision of
future society. There are no messianic or comprehensive theories
to provide it either with cohesion or with continuity of action.
The neo-proletariat is no more than a vague area made up of
constantly changing individuals whose main aim is not to seize
power in order to build a new world, but to regain power over
their own lives by disengaging from the market rationality of
productivism.

It cannot be otherwise. Society cannot be reconstructed by
decree, and a comprehensive vision has no meaning or purchase
unless it is an extension of an already developing process. But
the crisis of the industrial system heralds no new world. Nothing
in it is indicative of a redeeming transformation. The present
does not receive any meaning from the future. The silence of
history therefore returns individuals to themselves. Forced back
upon their own subjectivity, they have to take the floor on their
own behalf. No future society speaks through their mouth, since
the society disintegrating before our eyes heralds no new order.

The non-class engendered by the decomposition of present-day
society can only conceive of the non-society of which it is the
prefiguration. The term 'non-class' should not, of course, be
taken to imply the absence of social relations and social
organisation. It is used to designate the process of subtraction
from the social sphere of an area of individual sovereignty
beyond economic rationality and external constraint.

The primacy attached to individual sovereignty echoes that
revolutionary bourgeois thought which the bourgeoisie itself
rejected once it had obtained power. It flies in the face of or-
thodox socialist thinking, whose implicit premise has always
been that individuals should find personal fulfilment in the

appropriation of collective reality and in the common production of the social whole. In Marx there appeared to be some basis for this premise, in that he expected full development of the productive forces to engender fully developed individuals capable of appropriating the productive forces as a whole. It was assumed that there would be a continuum and an absence of conflict between individual activity and social production (and *vice versa*) The personalisation of social activity and the socialisation of personal activity were taken to be the two sides of communist development.

Marx's postulate has never been practically verified. The productive forces — or, to be more precise, production techniques — did not develop in such a way that socialised production (or socially necessary labour) could become an enriching personal activity, nor, above all, in such a way that the organisation and division of labour at the level of society as a whole could be controlled, reflected upon and experienced by each individual as the universally desired result of voluntary cooperation.

Everything now indicates that it is impossible to create a highly industrialised society (and hence a world order) which presents itself to each individual as the desired outcome of his or her free social cooperation with other individuals. There is a difference in both scale and nature between communal work or life and the social totality. Although it may be possible to build a highly conscious community through total personal involvement in cooperative activity, conflicts and affective relations, so that everyone assures the cohesion of what they feel to be 'their' community, society as a whole will still remain a system of relations embodied in and governed by institutional organisations, infrastructures of communication and production, and a geographical and social division of labour whose inertia is its guarantee of continuity and efficacy. As a structured system, society is necessarily external to its members. It is not the product of free, voluntary cooperation. Individuals do not produce it by starting from themselves: they produce it on the ground of its own inert exigencies, adapting themselves to the jobs, functions, skills, environments and hierarchical relations pre-established by society to assure its cohesive functioning.

This pre-establishment of 'socially necessary' activities is not the work of a subjective agent, a genius leader or Supreme

Guide, at least not in market societies. Planning committees, civil service departments, private and public technocracies and governments themselves certainly carry out the work of programming, regulating, forecasting and adjusting. Yet this manifold of collective, anonymous, conflictual and fragmented activities never crystallises into a comprehensive project under the personal direction of the head of the executive or the ruling political party. In other words, the cohesive workings of society appear to be assured, for good or ill, by a quasi-subject, the state. But the state is not a real subject: it is no one. In itself it is no more than an administrative machine, controlled by no one and incapable of formulating a general will which everyone may be called upon to express. The limits, dysfunctions and weaknesses of the capitalist state mean that society is always imperfectly cohesive and, as a result, that more or less substantial areas of indeterminacy and freedom will remain.

Since it advocates social integration not through the random play of multiple initiatives and conflicts, but through consciously willed planning or programming of the activity of society, socialist political theory implicitly gives society precedence over the individual and assumes their common subordination to the state. This latter is called upon to coordinate the global project of development whose imperatives are to be internalised by each and all as a common will and a social cement. In theory, the superiority of socialist society lies in the fact that the outcome of multiple activities is not, as in market societies, a random result which can only be corrected after the event either by the state or by individuals themselves, with all the waste, delay, duplication and error that this entails. The specificity of socialism lies in the fact that the results of social activity are determined in advance as an objective chosen by the collectivity, so that each person's activity is adapted, regulated and programmed as a function of this collective goal.

The problem, however, is precisely to define the collective goal. I shall return to this point in the next chapter. For the moment, let me simply note that whatever the process by which one or several collective projects are elaborated, and whatever the choice or choices of the type of society and culture they imply, it will always be a process that requires mediation and mediators. It cannot be undertaken by individuals as such, nor even by 'the associated producers', local communities or councils (soviets). It implies an overall vision of what society is to become — and even pluralism, a multiplication of decision-making centres, an increase in the space allowed to individual liberty, and careful limitation of the area encompassed by the state's sphere, amount to an overall vision. But even if such a vision is the result of genuinely democratic political debate involving parties and movements, its application will still entail planning, and planning requires a state.

Of course the elaboration of the plan may itself be hedged about with democratic safeguards. There may, for example, be broad consultation to establish the possibilities and preferences of each collective of producers, each local community, each region etc.; and several ups and downs to the coordinating body, back to the grass-roots community and vice versa to allow each to correct the other as the plan is carried out. Yet however open and sincerely democratic the process of consultation, the plan schedule and objectives will never be the expression of a common civic will or of grass-roots preferences. The mediations which made it possible to coordinate broad social options with grass-roots preferences will be so complex and so numerous that the local community will be unable to recognise itself in the final result. This result — the plan — will inevitably be the work of a state technocracy obliged to make use of mathematical models and statistical materials which in itself can only imperfectly control because of the very large number of inputs, variables and unforeseeable elements. Thus the plan will never be a 'photograph' of everyone's preferences, but will have to adjust each sub-set of preferences in the light of all the other sub-sets and of the technico-economic constraints upon their coherence. In the last analysis, 'democratic elaboration' of the plan does not allow each and all to become the subject of that voluntary social cooperation through which 'the associated producers' are supposed to impose their common will upon the society they seek to create. Instead, the plan remains an 'autonomised result', intended by no one and experienced by all as a set of external constraints.

From the point of view of the individual, the plan has no advantage over the market. It, too, expresses *an average* of heterogeneous preferences, which, like the 'average consumer' or the 'person in the street' of market surveys, does not correspond to the real preferences of real people. The person in the street never exists as self, only as 'the others'.[1]

In these circumstances, it is wrong to make it everyone's patriotic, civic or political duty to equate the objectives of the plan with his or her personal fulfilment. For that is to require an unconditional identity between individual and state, and an abandonment of the specificity and autonomy of all values and activities not related to politics and the economy. From being 'soldiers of production' in the capitalist economy, individuals end up as soldiers permanently mobilised to serve a plan presented to them as the emanation of 'the general will'. As long as the protagonists of socialism continue to make centralised planning (however much it might be broken down into local and regional plans) the linchpin of their programme, and the adherence of everyone to the 'democratically formulated' objectives of the plan the core of their political doctrine, socialism will remain an unattractive proposition in industrial societies.

The source of the theoretical superiority of socialism over capitalism is thus the source of its practical inferiority. To argue that society should be the controlled, programmed result of its members' activity is to demand that everyone should make their conduct functional to the overall social result in view. Thus, there can be no room for any form of conduct which, if generalised, would not lead to the programmed social outcome. Classical socialist doctrine finds it difficult to come to terms with political and social pluralism, understood not simply as a plurality of parties and trade unions but as the coexistence of various ways of working, producing and living, various and distinct cultural areas and levels of social existence.

Yet this kind of pluralism precisely conforms to the lived experience and aspirations of the post-industrial proletariat, as well as the major part of the traditional working class. Only by continually stressing and defending its importance can market societies maintain their legitimacy in the eyes of the majority of the population. And it is precisely because the socialist movement

---

1. This is an instance of what Sartre called serial alienation in the *Critique of Dialectical Reason*, London, New Left Books 1976.

has failed to embrace and enrich this pluralist perspective that it has condemned itself to a minority position even among working people.

Essentially, the 'freedom' which the majority of the population of the overdeveloped nations seeks to protect from 'collectivism' and the 'totalitarian' threat, is the freedom to create a private niche protecting one's personal life against all pressures and external social obligations. This niche may be represented by family life, a home of one's own, a back garden, a do-it-yourself workshop, a boat, a country cottage, a collection of antiques, music, gastronomy, sport, love etc. Its importance varies inversely with the degree of job satisfaction and in direct proportion with the intensity of social pressures. It represents a sphere of sovereignty wrested (or to be wrested) from a world governed by the principles of productivity, aggression, competition, hierarchical discipline etc. Capitalism owes its political stability to the fact that, in return for the dispossession and growing constraints experienced at work, individuals enjoy the possibility of building an *apparently* growing sphere of individual autonomy outside of work.

It is possible, following Rudolf Bahro, to regard this individual sphere as a sort of 'compensation' for the repression and frustration of the 'emancipatory needs'[2] and to conclude that such 'compensatory needs' will disappear after the 'general abolition of the condition of subordination' associated with the 'vertical division of labour'. This, however, is a dangerously simplistic view.[3] The sphere of individual sovereignty is *not based upon a mere desire to consume*, nor solely upon relaxation and leisure activities. It is based, more profoundly, upon activities unrelated to any economic goal which are an end in themselves: communication, giving, creating and aesthetic enjoyment, the production and reproduction of life, tenderness, the realisation

---

2. Rudolf Bahro, *The Alternative in Eastern Europe*, London, New Left Books 1978, pp.253 *et seq.*
3. Bahro's conception is actually very much more subtle since he posits individual self-realisation, even in socialised production, and the development of autonomous individual activities as the premises of the communist cultural revolution. In this he is strictly marxist, as we shall see. Cf. Bahro, *op.cit.* pp. 377 *et seq.*

of physical, sensuous and intellectual capacities, the creation of non-commodity use-values (shared goods or services) that could not be produced as commodities because of their unprofitability — in short, the whole range of activities that make up the fabric of existence and therefore occupy a primordial rather than a subordinate place. An inversion of the scale of priorities, involving a subordination of socialised work governed by the economy to activities constituting the sphere of individual autonomy, is underway in every class within the over-developed societies and particularly among the post-industrial neo-proletariat.[4] 'Real life' begins outside of work, and work itself has become a means towards the extension of the sphere of non-work, a temporary occupation by which individuals acquire the possibility of pursuing their main activities. This is a cultural mutation announcing the transition to post-industrial society. It implies a radical subversion of the ideology, scale of values and social relations established by capitalism. But it will only eliminate capitalism if its latent content is revealed in the form of an alternative to capitalism that is able to capture the developing cultural mutation and give it political extension.

The idea that economically oriented social labour should serve to extend the sphere of individual autonomy — meaning free-time activity — was already central in Marx's thought. Its realisation was synonymous with the advent of communism and the extinction of political economy.[5] Pan-economism, or the

---

4. See Appendix 1 below.
5. 'As soon as labour in the direct form has ceased to be the great well-spring of wealth, labour time ceases and must cease to be its measure, and hence exchange value [must cease to be the measure] of use value... With that, production based on exchange value breaks down, and the direct, material production process is stripped of the form of penury and antithesis. The free development of individualities, and hence... the general reduction of the necessary labour of society to a minimum, which then corresponds to the artistic, scientific etc. development of the individuals in the time set free, and with the means created, for all of them.' (*Grundrisse*, Harmondsworth, Penguin 1973, pp.705-6.) And Marx goes on to cite an astonishing unsigned work entitled *The Source and Remedy*, published in 1821:

Truly wealthy a nation, when the working day is 6 rather than 12 hours. *Wealth* is not command over surplus labour time, but rather, *disposable time* outside that needed in direct production, for *every*

subordination of every activity to those associated with the economy, is specific to capitalist development. Only with capitalism does work, or the heteronomous production of exchange-values, become a full-time activity and the self-supply of goods and services (by the family or community) become a marginal and subordinate activity. An inversion of this relationship will signify the end of political economy and the advent of 'post-industrial socialism' or communism.

It is an inversion already underway, although this has been more or less successfully concealed by the dominant system. In fact the hegemony of economic rationality has never been total. As feminist theorists have indicated, the sphere of commodity production could never have existed without a parallel sphere of household production not subject to economic rationality. In particular, all activities associated with the reproduction of life are outside the domain of economic rationality — as are the majority of aesthetic and pedagogic activities. Raising children, looking after and decorating a house, repairing or making things, cooking good meals, entertaining guests, listening to or performing music — none of these activities is carried out for economic ends or for consumption. This extra-economic sphere, by no means necessarily confined to the home or the nuclear family, has in practice always been as important as the sphere of economic production, providing it with a concealed material base through the unremunerated and unmeasured housework of women and, to a lesser extent, of children and grandparents.

Such work has never been recognised in capitalist society. Because it does not create a surplus that can be accumulated or sold on the market, it has never been defined as *work*, but seen as a sort of personal service without economic value.[6] For some theorists of the women's movement, housework is therefore an enclave of slave labour within the capitalist economy. The

individual and the whole society.
(Chicago, University of Chicago Press 1958.)
6. In *The Human Condition*, Hannah Arendt has produced an excellent account of how, from the Greeks to the present, the notion of productive labour has ignored all those types of work (such as cleaning, maintenance, mending, etc.) whose results cannot be stored or accumulated. All these types of tasks, which have to be repeated day after day, were formerly consigned to slaves.

bourgeoisie may have abolished slavery in relations between workers and bosses, but it has not done so in the relations between men and women. According to this interpretation, it is only right to extend market regulations to the sphere of housework, integrating it into the sector of activity governed by economic ends. Housework should be waged, to the extent that it cannot be industrialised.

The only value of this uselessly simplistic and regressive theory lies in its demonstration, carried to absurd lengths, that the autonomous activities of the extra-economic sphere fall outside any possible economic rationalisation. Political economy here reaches its limits. Indeed, if housework were remunerated at the marginal price of an hour's work — so that the performance of an hour's housework entitled the person in question to receive the quantity of goods and services that could be produced in one hour in the commodity sector — the cost of domestic payments would be so high as to exceed the capacities of even the most opulent society.[7]

This example is even more suggestive for its non-economic implications than for its economic significance. If the activities performed by women without any financial reward were to be given a wage, they would either not be done at all or would be done very differently. All the aspects of 'spontaneous offering', affective involvement and scrupulous care would not only

---

7. Andret, in *Travailler deux heures par jour*, Editions du Seuil 1977, gives the following proportions for 'captive' and 'free' work (i.e. waged and unwaged work) in present-day France: 60% for unwaged work and 40% for waged work. This distribution of the total number of waged and unwaged hours of work is very unequal, given the sexual division of labour: 24.5 billion hours of waged work for men and 12.7 billion for women, while men carry out 9 billion hours of unpaid work and women some 40 billion.

All of this indicates that the unpaid work carried out by women (mainly as housework) is in fact captive and will only become a genuinely free activity when women are no longer responsible for four-fifths of household tasks:

In a society in which everyone has the time and is accustomed to taking a turn, housework will be shared by all. It will recover its meaning as a symbol of the mutual exchange of affection, of collective responsibility for the concrete aspects of communal life and as an opportunity to enjoy tasks which, when carried out by the same individual every day, become profoundly tedious.

(Andret, *op.cit.* pp.114-15)

become 'priceless', but could never in fact be expected of a male or female wage worker whose main concern was to exchange a certain number of working hours for market goods and services of an equivalent value.

Besides, the search for higher productivity would lead to the standardisation and industrialisation of such activities, particularly those involving the feeding, minding, raising and education of children. The last enclave of individual or communal autonomy would disappear; socialisation, 'commodification' and pre-programming would be extended to the last vestiges of self-determined and self-regulated life. The industrialisation, through home computers, of physical and psychical care and hygiene, children's education, cooking or sexual technique is precisely designed to generate capitalist profits from activities still left to individual fantasy.[8] It is leading towards that social *trivialisation*[9] of the most intimate areas of individual behaviour which Jacques Attali has described as the 'society of self-supervision'.[10]

The computerised socialisation of autonomous activities runs directly against the aspirations at work in post-industrial society. Instead of enlarging the sphere of individual autonomy, it can only subordinate the activities constituting this sphere to the productivist criteria of profitability, speed and conformity to the norm. At the very moment when the reduction in socially necessary labour time is increasing free time and the possibilities for individual fulfilment in non-economic activity, computerised socialisation seeks to reduce this time. Its development implies the 'liberation' of individuals from their freely chosen activities, in order to reduce them, even in the domestic field, to passive users of commodity objects, information and programmes.

The women's movement enters the logic of capital when it seeks to free women from non-economically oriented activities by defining these as servile, subordinate tasks which need to be abolished. They are servile and subordinate, however, only to the extent that economically oriented activities remain dominant

---

8. A Gorz. *Ecology as Politics*, Boston, South End Press 1980, pp.77 *et seq*.
9. 'Trivial' is used by Heinz von Foerster to denote the perfectly predictable responses produced by a system (either living or mechanical) to a given stimulus.
10. In *La Nouvelle Economie Française*, Paris, Flammarion 1978.

(and endowed with 'noble' status) both in society and in the household community itself. This dominance is precisely what is being called into question. Only *insofar as* the women's movement deepens that challenge, asserting the centrality of non-economic values and autonomous activities, and the subordination of economic values and activities, will it become a dynamic component of the post-industrial revolution and, in many respects, its vanguard. From this perspective, its main concern can no longer be that of liberating women from housework but of extending the non-economic rationality of these activities beyond the home. It has to win over men both inside and outside the home; to subvert the traditional sexual division of labour; and to abolish not only the hegemony of the values of virility but these values themselves, both in relations between the sexes and in society at large. Thus, as Herbert Marcuse has shown, post-industrial socialism — that is communism — will be female or will not exist at all.[11] This implies a cultural revolution which will eliminate the principle of performance, the ethic of competition, accumulation and the rat-race at the level of both individual behaviour and social relations, replacing them with the supremacy of the values of reciprocity, tenderness, spontaneity and love of life in all its forms.

In this respect, as Alain Touraine has said, the women's movement is,

> a movement of liberation not only *of* women but of men *by* women. One of its most basic aspects is its opposition to military and financial models of organisation, to the power of money and giant organisations. It represents a will to organise one's own life, to form personal relationships, to love and be loved, to have a child. Of all social movements, the women's movement is the one most able to oppose the growing hold exercised by giant corporations over our daily lives. Only women have preserved those personal qualities which male domination has crushed out of men. Since they have been completely excluded from political and

11. Herbert Marcuse, 'Marxisme et féminisme', in *Actuels*, Paris, Galilée 1975.

> military power, women have succeeded in maintaining
> a capacity for affective relations from which men have
> been estranged by the structures of power — or have
> estranged themselves to serve the structures.
>
> Thanks to the women's movement, we men have
> already regained certain rights to express feelings, to
> get involved with children, and so on. What began as a
> form of cultural self-defence can become a directly
> social and political struggle against a world of
> managers, sub-managers and employees, and against
> all aspects of a life wholly devoted to keeping the
> machine in motion.[12]

Thus, far from being a relic of pre-capitalist society, women's
activities and qualities prefigure a post-capitalist and post-
industrial society, culture and civilisation. Indeed, in every
overdeveloped society they are already imposing their ethical
hegemony in relations between couples. The qualities and values
of women are becoming common to men and women, particularly, but not exclusively, among the post-industrial proletariat.
Taking care of babies is no longer exclusively allocated to
women, just as full-time socialised work is no longer the
prerogative of a male 'bread-winner'. The ever more frequent
permutation of tasks and roles within the extended or nuclear
family is abolishing not only sexual but other hierarchies: wage
labour no longer seems more 'noble' or admirable than unpaid,
autonomous activity within the extended or nuclear family.
People can find greater fulfilment in the latter than in the
former.

It is also far from true that the increasingly secondary
character of wage labour and economic goals encourages individuals to accept any type of work or working conditions
without a murmur. The opposite is the case. Growing personal
fulfilment results in greater demands and growing combativeness
rather than resigned indifference. The more people are capable
of practical and affective autonomy, the less they are willing to
accept hierarchical discipline and the more demanding they

---

12. Alain Touraine, 'La révolution culturelle que nous vivons', *Le Nouvel
Observateur* 1 August 1978.

become as regards both the quality and the content of the work required of them.[13]

The priority task of a post-industrial left must therefore be to extend self-motivated, self-rewarding activity within, and above all, outside the family, and to limit as much as possible all waged or market-based activity carried out on behalf of third parties (even the state). A reduction in work time is a necessary but not a sufficient condition. For it will not help to enlarge the sphere of individual autonomy if the resulting free time remains empty 'leisure time', filled for better or worse by the programmed distractions of the mass media and the oblivion merchants, and if everyone is thereby driven back into the solitude of their private sphere.

More than upon free time, the expansion of the sphere of autonomy depends upon a freely available supply of convivial tools that allow individuals to do or make anything whose aesthetic or use-value is enhanced by doing it oneself. Repair and do-it-yourself workshops in blocks of flats, neighbourhood centres or rural communities should enable everyone to make or invent things as they wish. Similarly, libraries, places to make music or movies, 'free' radio and television stations, open spaces for communication, circulation and exchange, and so on[14] need to be accessible to everyone.

The extraordinary success (particularly in Germany) of Bahro's book *The Alternative in Eastern Europe* is mainly due to the manner in which he has revived a dimension of marxist thought[15] ignored in socialist or 'communist' policies and programmes (apart, that is, from various dissident Italian groups, running from Il Manifesto to the various 'autonomist'

---

13. See the account given by Charly Boyadjian in *Travailler deux heures par jour*, *op.cit.* where the monotony and stupidity of work become the more apparent as the length of the working week becomes shorter and where, because of partial unemployment, family life and affective relationships are able to grow. The accounts presented in this work all demonstrate the accuracy of Simone Weil's remark that 'no one would accept being a slave for two hours a day.' See also the classic studies by Kornhauser, showing that anomie varies inversely with the possibility of personal involvement in one's work: A. Kornhauser, *Mental Health of the Industrial Worker*, New York, Wiley 1965.
14. See Appendix 2 below.
15. A dimension that is particularly visible in the *Grundrisse*.

currents).[16] In this dimension, communism is conceived as the extinction of political economy, and as the measurement of wealth by freely determined possibilities for happiness rather than quantities of exchange-value.

> *One* of the essential preconditions for a cultural-revolutionary economic policy is a theory of development of human individuality, dominated neither by a fetishism of 'objective requirements', nor by the impressive adaptability of the psyche, and daring to make normative assertions. The communist demand, in short, is that the overall production and reproduction of material life should be reshaped in such a way that people be repaid for their work as individuals.
>
> If a society is so far industrialised that it can fairly reliably satisfy the elementary needs of its members at the level of culture that has been attained, then the planning of the overall process of reproduction must... give *priority* to the all-round development of human beings, to the increase in their positive capacities for happiness... Historical examples show, moreover, that the same or similar results of human development and human happiness are compatible with fairly great differences in the quantity of available products. In no case can the conditions for freedom be measured in dollars or roubles per head. What people in the developed countries need is not the extension of their present needs, but rather the opportunity for self-enjoyment in doing, enjoyment in personal relations, concrete life in the broadest sense. The remoulding of the process of socialisation in this direction will be characterised first of all at the economic base by a

---

16. Notably Antonio Negri who writes, in his commentary on the *Grundrisse*:

    Communism can only be equated with planning to the extent to which it is firstly defined in terms of the abolition of work... When the preconditions and the aim of the abolition of work do not exist, planning can only be a new form of capitalist command — its socialist form.
    (A. Negri, *Marx au-delà de Marx*, Paris, Christian Bourgois 1979, pp.288-89)

systematic restructuring of living labour and accumulation, in favour of the conditions helping the unfolding of human subjectivity.

Among these conditions are 'the re-establishment of proportionality between large-scale (industrial) and small-scale (handicraft) production'.

The production of surplus consciousness that is already in train spontaneously must be vigorously pursued in an active way, so as to produce quite intentionally a surplus of education which is so great, both quantitatively and qualitatively, that it cannot possibly be trapped in the existing structures of work and leisure time, so that the contradictions of these structures come to a head and their revolutionary transformation becomes indispensable.[17]

---

17. Rudolf Bahro, *op.cit*. pp.404 *et seq*. Bahro, who is not a 'dissident', was responsible for training industrial management in East Germany.

8. Towards a Dual Society

Material necessities and moral exigency

Contrary to what Marx thought, it is impossible that individuals should totally coincide with their social being,[1] or that social being should encompass all the dimensions of individual existence. Individual existence can never be entirely socialised. It involves areas of experience which, being essentially secret, intimate, unmediated and incapable of mediation, can never be had in common. There can be no socialisation of tenderness, love, creativity, aesthetic pleasure (or ecstasy), suffering, mourning or anguish;[2] nor, conversely, any personalisation of necessities which derive from the coexistence of individuals in one and the same material field, where each individual's behaviour is ruled by physical laws.[3]

Insofar as they have postulated that individuals exhaustively coincide with their social being, and that social being realises the full wealth of human capacities, the theories, utopian visions and political practices of socialism have led to a straightforward negation of the individual subject. By negating singularity,

---

1. In his early philosophical works, especially the *1844 Manuscripts*, *The Critique of the Philosophy of Right* 1843, and *The German Ideology*. See *Collected Works*, London, Lawrence & Wishart.
2. The socialised forms of these relations are always a conventionalised or ritualised substitution for subjective profundity, designed either to console, compensate or repress. Cf A. Gorz, *Fondements pour une Morale*, Paris, Galilée 1977, pp. 541-55, 589.
3. The most notable examples are the physical laws governing every type of serial process, such as the circulation of traffic or money, the maintenance of giant industrial or urban systems etc. in which individuals function like a mass of molecules governed by the dynamic of fluids. The passenger on the 8.30 train, the cashier or the meter-reader are never persons in their roles as passenger, cashier etc. but only beyond or outside their serial social being.

subjectivity, doubt, and that area of silence and incommunicability peculiar to affective life, they imply the repression of everything — from the lovers' wish for solitude to artistic or intellectual creation which remains intractable to universalisation or normalisation. They have resulted in the persecution and, in extreme cases, the extermination of people who have resisted the total socialisation of individuality or have remained aware of its failure.

This repressive, inquisitorial, normalising and conformist quality is something that socialist morality has had in common with the social moralities of religious communities, catholic fundamentalism, and military or fascist societies. This has been so because any morality which takes the universal (and the good) as a given, deducing from it what individuals must do and be, is bound to be oppressive and dogmatic. The result is an amoralism, a passion for order in which, as Hegel remarked, 'the absolute purpose is that moral action do not take place at all'.[4] For no morality is possible unless the subject — individual conscience — is taken as the point of departure. If conscience is not the determining instance of what I can or must do or be, then morality becomes a function of the requirements of the social order, and everyone is required to be and do what society needs.

As a system of material relations, society has laws of functioning and material constraints that are not guaranteed by some pre-established harmony to be in conformity, or even compatible, with moral exigency. Particularly in complex, industrialised societies, where social relations are mediated and structured by large-scale structures, socially necessary activities are necessary not to self-based responsible individuals but to a material system that still has the character of a huge machine. The functions or work carried out by a traffic warden, road-sweeper, tax-inspector, computer operator, postal sorter or court attendant are determined by the requirements of the social system rather than by ethical rules. Each of these heteronomous activities is the result of 'external necessity', not of a purpose chosen by the

---

4. G.W.F. Hegel, 'Spirit Certain of Itself', *The Phenomenology of Mind* (tr. Baillie), London, Allen & Unwin 1966, p. 632.

individuals themselves. They are all governed by rigid rules and regulations designed to ensure that individuals *function* like mere machines, so that their actions can be synchronised in such a way as to produce the intended effect.

The rules, regulations and laws of a complex society dominated by large-scale structures are the result of technical imperatives. They serve to define technical, not moral behaviour. Their purpose and effect is to objectify the action expected of each person, encoding it as something prior and external to the actor. Individuals are held responsible not for the predetermined action itself, but merely for good or bad observation of the rules and regulations. Personal responsibility is thus effectively abolished or (in the case of soldiers, civil servants and all subordinate functionaries) it is prohibited. Rules are 'not for discussion'; 'good' executive officers will say: 'We're just doing our job', or 'I'm just following orders' — which is a way of refusing all personal responsibility for what they do.

Every social order, particularly the socialism of scarcity, tends to equate morality with obedience to rules and regulations, as if these were ethical injunctions rather than technical means, often provisional and improvised, of ensuring the operation of a contingent material system. Socialist state morality, like military or technocratic morality, has so far consisted of an injunction that individuals should identify with the heteronomous functions and modes of behaviour whose nature is defined by the workings of society as a material system or 'apparatus'. A technical imperative has thus simply replaced all ethical exigencies. Emergency conditions are put forward to bar any criticism or transformation of the structures. The materiality of the technical relations they determine becomes the measure of how interpersonal and social relations 'must be'. In the last analysis, the foundations of morality are the technical requirements of the social machine — with the state as its chief engineer (and the political police as its clergy).

One can research this system in vain for an area in which moral agency can be found. It is not present at the level of individual relations, nor at the level of a state order which, though supposed to embody the supreme good, actually is but the workings of mechanisms and apparatuses operating entirely beyond any political, social or individual will and control.

In this totalitarian context, individual consciousness reveals itself sub rosa as the sole possible foundation of morality. Moral consciousness always arises through an act of rebellion, the very moment when an individual refuses to obey by stating, 'I can't. Not that.' This refusal is the cornerstone of moral exigency, its *cogito*. It is a revolt against the realism of 'objective morality', in the name of a realism of an entirely different order which asserts as impossible the idea that an individual cannot be the sovereign judge of what should and should not be done.

The moment of ethical awareness may be summarised in the question, 'Can I want that?' — meaning, 'Can I, in my own name, want that action in both its form and its consequences? Could I, in doing it, say: That's what I wanted to do, I answer for it?'

The specific characteristic of 'objective morality' is that it exempts individuals from asking this type of question. Theirs is not to seek or to doubt. To be assured of the good, all they need to do is obey; the authorities, or history, or the party or the church will take responsibility. In other words, 'objective morality' does not expect subjectivity from individuals. And with the disappearance of subjectivity, morality itself is bound to disappear since the meaning and value of human ends is no longer posed. The question is no longer whether I can want to do what I am doing, merely whether 'it's necessary'. People always become anti-human in the name of some inescapable necessity. I term alienation the impossibility of willing what one does, or of producing acts that can be taken as ends both in their results and in the forms of their accomplishment.[5] An alienated individual's reply to the moral question, 'Can I want to do that?', will always be, 'It isn't me...'; 'It had to be...'; 'There was no other choice...' etc.

There can be neither morality nor relations informed by morality unless two conditions are fulfilled. First, there must exist a sphere of autonomous activity in which the individual is the sovereign author of actions carried out without recourse to necessity, alibis or excuses. Secondly, this sphere must be prevalent, rather than subordinate, in the process whereby

---

5. A. Gorz, *op.cit.*

individuals freely produce themselves and the web of their relations with others.

Nevertheless, as we shall see, the sphere of autonomy cannot embrace everything. It could only do so if its constituent community, founded upon self-regulating, reciprocal relations, were to cover the whole world; or if the world were of the same size as that community and devoid of scarcity, forces hostile to human life and constraints of any kind. Both are impossible. In Marx, the reappropriation of the entire world, as an entity made transparent by and for everyone, was predicated not only upon abundance but also, as Pierre Rosanvallon has shown, upon the idea of a simple, unmediated family-like community, coextensive with humanity as a whole.[6] Inversely, neo-utopian visions of 'retribalisation', like the ideal micro-societies dreamt in the late Middle Ages or the Renaissance, presuppose the creation of self-sufficient communities outside the world and history, protected from external corruption by their physical isolation.

Either perspective leads to a form of pseudo-moralism which, by seeking to eliminate everything that cannot be produced, planned and controlled by sovereign individuals themselves, forces them into one of two equally untenable positions. In the one instance individuals pretend to work by their own free will realities which in fact are beyond their control and possible self-determination. This is the peculiar characteristic of the communist passion. Alternatively, by wilfully ignoring the outside world, individuals abandon all control over the way their ideal community is inserted into and utilised by the dominant social order.

Practical autonomy and heteronomy: the two spheres

Making morality prevail does not necessarily require the suppression of the sphere of heteronomy. It merely requires its subordination to the sphere of autonomy. This in turn will be guaranteed to the extent that all-round individual development through autonomous activities and relations becomes the effective goal which social institutions and their irreducible core of

---

6. Pierre Rosanvallon, *Le capitalisme utopique*, Paris, Editions du Seuil 1979.

heteronomous activities are made to serve.

Marx already envisaged that, at the end of volume 3 of *Capital*, when he described how the 'sphere of freedom' (or autonomy) would only begin beyond a 'sphere of necessity' (or heteronomy) that could be reduced but never entirely eliminated. By recognising its inevitability, not by denying its existence, will it be possible to reduce its importance as much as possible and, as a result, ensure that its logic does not dominate every type of individual activity.

> In fact, the realm of freedom actually begins only where labour which is determined by necessity and mundane considerations ceases; thus in the nature of things it lies beyond the sphere of actual material production. Just as the savage must wrestle with Nature to satisfy his wants, to maintain and reproduce life, so must civilised man, and he must do so in all social formations and under all possible modes of production. With his development this realm of physical necessity expands as a result of his wants; but, at the same time, the forces of production which satisfy these needs also develop. Freedom in this field can only consist in socialised man, the associated producers, rationally regulating their interchange with Nature, bringing it under their common control, instead of being ruled by it as by the blind forces of Nature; and achieving this with the least expenditure of energy and under conditions most favourable to, and worthy of, their human nature. But it nonetheless remains a realm of necessity. Beyond it begins that development of human energy which is an end in itself, the true realm of freedom, which, however, can blossom forth only with this realm of necessity as its basis. The shortening of the working-day is its basic prerequisite.[7]

It will be apparent that, contrary to a widespread misconception, Marx does not equate the reign of liberty with self-management of material production by the associated producers.

---

7. K. Marx, *Capital*, vol.3, London, Lawrence & Wishart, p. 820.

In fact he asserts that material production is subject to natural necessities (of which the physical laws of large machinery are one) and that, *at the level of material production*, freedom consists merely of being able to work with as much dignity and efficiency as possible for as brief a time as possible. This is the direction in which self-management should point. As for the realm of freedom, it will flourish through the reduction of working time and of the effort involved in producing what is necessary.

In short, there can only be a twofold solution, involving the organisation of a discontinuous social space made up of two distinct spheres, and a rhythm of life governed by the passage from the one to the other.

The same type of institution may be found in the work of Ivan Illich. Far from calling for the abolition of industrial work and production, he sets out the case for a synergic relation between the heteronomous and autonomous modes of production, aiming at the utmost expansion of the sphere of autonomy. This may be facilitated by complex tools and advanced technologies, despite the fact that they imply heteronomous work. It would be wrong to reject such developments if, at the same time, they allow everyone access to 'convivial tools' which

> can be easily used, by anybody, as often or as seldom as desired, for the accomplishment of a purpose chosen by the user. The use of such tools by one person does not restrain another from using them equally.

'In principle,' Illich continues,

> the distinction between convivial and manipulatory tools is independent of the level of technology of the tool. What has been said of the telephone could be repeated point by point for the mails or for a typical Mexican market. Each is an institutional arrangement that maximises liberty, even though in a broader context it can be abused for purposes of manipulation and control.
>
> It is possible that not every means of desirable production in a post-industrial society would fit the criteria of conviviality... It is almost certain that in a

period of transition from the present to the future mode of production in certain countries, electricity would not commonly be produced in the backyard... What is fundamental to a convivial society is not the total absence of manipulative institutions and addictive goods and services, but the balance between those tools which create the specific demands they are specialised to satisfy and those complementary, enabling tools which foster self-realisation. The first set of tools produces according to abstract plans for men in general; the other set enhances the ability of people to pursue their own goals in their unique way.[8]

I have attempted elsewhere to illustrate a dual organisation of social space into a heteronomous sphere subordinate to the objectives of the sphere of autonomy.[9] The former assures the programmed and planned production of everything necessary to individual and social life, with the maximum efficiency and the least expenditure of effort and resources. In the latter sphere, individuals autonomously produce non-necessary material and non-material goods and services, outside of the market, by themselves or in free association with others, and in conformity with their own desires, tastes or fantasies. With primary needs satisfied, the wealth of society is measured by the variety and abundance of convivial tools permanently available in workshops for everyone's use, in local communities, districts, neighbourhood centres or blocks of flats.

It is thus made possible for individuals to move continually between heteronomous, wage-based social labour in the general interest, requiring little time or intense personal involvement, and autonomous activities which carry their end in themselves. This naturally encourages people to become extremely critical and demanding of the nature and finality of socially necessary labour. But it also frees them from the compulsion to seek a social identity or personal fulfilment in this type of heteronomous activity. In other words, the realm of moral exigency is virtually

8. I. Illich, *Tools for Conviviality*, London, Calder and Boyars 1973, pp. 22-24.
9. See Appendix 2 below, reproducing a text already published in A. Gorz, *Ecology as Politics*, Boston, South End Press 1980.

disconnected from that of objective necessities of a material or technical sort. Individuals are free to see their socially necessary labour as a clearly demarcated external necessity taking but a marginal portion of their lives. They also, however, are free to seek personal fulfilment in and through socialised labour. And nothing prevents them from attaching equal importance to their socially determined and their autonomous activities; from striking a balance that is all the happier to the extent that the qualitative difference between the two is more marked. One could envisage such alternation over daily, weekly, seasonal or annual cycles, or according to the needs of different kinds or periods of life.[10]

This dual conception of society is now the only realistic and practicable solution. For although necessary production time may be very considerably reduced for each individual, it is not possible to make *every* type of socially necessary labour enjoyable or enriching for those called upon to carry it out. It is possible to enlarge the non-market field of autonomous, self-managed and self-motivated activity, encouraging auto-centred production and training, and replacing some of the services currently supplied by commercial organisations or bureaucratic administrations with mutual aid, cooperation and sharing. Yet it is not possible to self-manage the entire social process of production, nor even the large-scale technical units which make it up.

There are a number of reasons for this latter fact. Most crucially, the socialisation of production and of the productive forces has inevitably led to a decline of the old individual trades and the appearance of more narrowly specialised social skills. This process is irreversible. It has been accelerated rather than slowed down by automation. It is true that *technical* self-management of the labour process at the level of workshops, assembly units, offices or building sites makes it possible to improve the conditions, forms and relations of work. It may ensure that work is no longer crippling, exhausting and brutalising. It can give workers the power to regulate their own work rhythm, and to choose between such variables as the duration, intensity,

---

10. See Guy Aznar, *Non aux loisirs, non à la retraite*, Paris, Galilée 1978.

complexity and relative interest of work. (The most exhausting tasks are not necessarily the most complex or the most time-consuming.) But technical self-management will never allow individuals to find complete involvement and satisfaction in every type of socially determined activity. It is unable to halt the trend towards the abolition of old skills in the sphere of social production.

The old trades were often much more an *art* than a transmissible social skill. The 'know-how' of master craftsworkers was a *personal* capacity developed during a lifetime in a trade. The craft was something that each craftsworker kept improving: learning and progress never come to an end, new skills were acquired and tools perfected. Since a 'lifetime' was needed to learn a trade, each individual had to reinvent it on the basis of existing technology, so that the skills in question were never entirely codified or transmissible.

Social skills, on the other hand, involve the acquisition of given amounts of socialised and standardised knowledge. Such knowledge, which almost anyone can acquire in a certain period of time, is in principle common to all workers in a particular occupation. Apart from a few imponderables, their performances are therefore equivalent and interchangeable. Being, in principle, wholly communicated through instruction, such knowledge can never be the same as the *specific*, autonomous, self-improving know-how of the traditional craftsworker. Social skills do not therefore really belong to particular individuals. They are predetermined and limited both in their scope and their nature. Instead of belonging to individual members of a 'trade', they are the means by which people accede to membership of an economic and social system whose technological development and division of labour remain outside their control. In other words, a 'trade' no longer has any use-value for the individuals practising it. Largely external to them, it is fundamentally nothing more than their mode of insertion into the heteronomous system of giant scientific, technological or administrative structures whose complexity surpasses any one person's understanding. These can only function through the synchronisation of a mass of fragmented and complementary capacities, programmed for a result that transcends everyone.

Social skills therefore leave very little scope for development by the individual. Unless one is employed in high-level research or in sectors that still have a craft base, the inability to improve one's tools or to invent new ways of doing things virtually rules out any individual advance in the 'trade'. Instead of growing cumulatively richer, as in the old trades, social skills generally remain determined by the overall development of stocks of socialised knowledge throughout one's 'professional life'. Development of this kind — usually termed 'innovation' — is only rarely the work of individual subjects, or of a creative insight produced by someone 'in the trade' seeking to improve existing tools. Instead, it usually emanates from research departments in which almost everyone is engaged in fragmented work.

The division of labour is thus inevitably depersonalising. It turns work into a heteronomous activity, confining self-management to control over the effects of changes and decisions taken at a higher point of the production chain. Workers further down the chain can never make any decisive alteration. There can never be effective self-management of a big factory, an industrial combine or a bureaucratic department. It will always be defeated by the rigidity of technical constraints, and by the number of mediations between the wishes of 'those at the bottom' and the results of the job-study and methods departments.

It is thus impossible to abolish the depersonalisation, standardisation and trivialisation of socially determined labour without abolishing the division of labour through a return to craft production and the village economy. This is out of the question — and, contrary to an opinion widely held among those who have never read him, Illich himself has never suggested it. The division of labour and knowledge into fragmented but complementary technical skills is the only means by which it is possible to accumulate and put to work the huge stocks of knowledge embodied in machines, industrial systems and processes of every scale and dimension. Nothing can support the belief that convivial tools able to assure the autonomous production of use-values can or should be supplied by the autonomous sphere of production itself. Indeed, the more such tools embody concentrated masses of complex socialised knowledge in a form to be easily handled by everyone, the more extensive will be the sphere of autonomy. It is impossible to imagine that telephones, video machines, microprocessors, bicycles or photoelectric cells — all potentially convivial tools that can be put to autonomous purposes — could be produced at the level of a family, a group or a local community.

The point, then, is not to abolish heteronomous work, but only to use the goods it supplies and the way in which they are produced in order to enlarge the sphere of autonomy. It will serve that purpose all the better if it supplies the autonomous sphere with the greatest possible number of efficient convivial tools, and if the amount of heteronomous work required of each individual is reduced to a minimum. The existence of a sector of socialised production is thus indispensable for three basic reasons.

First, only the socialisation of knowledge, and of its storage and transmission, allows a plentiful supply of technologically advanced tools.

Second, the highly productive machinery capable of turning out such tools at low cost (whether they be cathode tubes or ball-bearings) is beyond the means of local communities or towns.

Third, if the time spent on heteronomous labour is to be reduced to a minimum, then everyone will have to do some work. But everyone can only work efficiently in the sector of heteronomous production if the complex knowledge required for the efficient execution of their tasks is embodied in industrial processes and stored in sophisticated machinery, so that the (social) skills needed for each activity can be acquired in a short period of time. Only standardised simplification allows the mass of socially necessary labour to be distributed among the population as a whole in such a way that the average working day is reduced to a few hours.

The extension of the sphere of autonomy is thus predicated upon a sphere of heteronomous production which, though industrialised, is restricted to socially necessary goods and services that cannot be supplied in an autonomous manner with the same efficacy.[11] Most of the objects in current use will therefore be best produced in long industrial runs, while most non-utilitarian

---

11. Understood in the double sense of *efficiency* (the yield in relation to the amount of energy expended) and *effectiveness* (the degree of conformity to the desired outcome).

objects will be best produced in the autonomous sphere. Heteronomous production may, for example, supply a limited range of sturdy, functional shoes and clothing with an optimal use-value, while an unlimited range of similar goods corresponding to individual tastes will be produced outside the market in communal workshops.[12] Inversely, only high-technology treatment will be provided in the industrialised hospital centres. The ordinary complaints which account for the immense majority of illnesses will be best treated at home with, if necessary, the help of relatives, friends or neighbours.

This dual organisation of social space into a heteronomous sphere made up of socially predetermined and relatively impersonal tasks, and an autonomous sphere in which 'anything goes', must not be thought of as a separation of the one from the other. Each sphere will, in fact, have repercussions on the other. The personal fulfilment, creativity and shared activity of the autonomous sector will stiffen people against the hierarchical division of labour and the production of goods of doubtful utility. Inversely, the socially determined nature of the heteronomous sphere will protect individuals from the pressures and tensions of highly integrated communities, whether formed by the family or by any other type of commune or cooperative association. We shall discuss this point at greater length in the next chapter.

What matters here is that the existence of a socialised sector of standard, simplified work will raise individuals above the narrow space of the local community and ensure that it does not drift towards autarky and self-sufficiency. For communal autarky always has an impoverishing effect: the more self-sufficient and numerically limited a community is, the smaller the range of activities and choices it can offer to its members. If it has no opening to an area of exogenous activity, knowledge and production, the community becomes a prison — exploitation by the family amounts to exploitation of the family. Only constantly renewed possibilities for discovery, insight, experiment and communication can prevent communal life from becoming impoverished and eventually suffocating. Precisely because of its heteronomous nature, socially determined labour provides

12. For more details, see Appendix 2.

the space for circulation on which communal life can feed. There is an obvious analogy here to the position of 'housewives' who see work outside the home as a liberation, even if most of the jobs on offer are particularly oppressive and one-sided.

All activities are impoverishing when they cannot be alternated with activities drawing upon other mental and physical energies. Heteronomous activity is impoverishing when it is done full-time to the exclusion of all others, and the same is true of autonomous activity. As Guy Aznar has said, no one can be creative for 12 hours a day, 365 days a years.[13] Regular to-ing and fro-ing between activities requiring intense personal involvement and work divested of mental and emotional effort is a source of balance and fulfilment.

The impossibility of abolishing heteronomous work is not then a bad thing in itself, provided that no one is forced to spend a lifetime engaged in some unrewarding and monotonous work.

Nor should anything prevent socially necessary labour from being an opportunity for festivity, pleasure and communication. *Culture* is, after all, no more than the over-determination of the necessary by the optional and the superfluous — a process which invests the material imperative with the transcendent aesthetic sense.

Work that is oppressive when carried out all day every day (like sorting the mail, collecting the rubbish, cleaning and repairing) could be no more than a brief interval among so many others if it was distributed among the whole population and therefore took only 15 minutes a day. It could even become a welcome distraction and opportunity for pleasure if, as is already the case with some types of agricultural or forestry work, it were to occupy only a few days a year or a few months in a lifetime.

Freedom cannot be based upon abolition of socially determined labour, nor (as will be argued more fully in the next chapter) upon elimination of external compulsion so as to have each individual perform what is objectively necessary as an internalised moral duty. Freedom consists in recognising that the sphere of necessity imposes certain heteronomous tasks whose technical

---

13. *op.cit.* note 10.

imperatives have nothing whatsoever to do with morality, and in confining such tasks to a specific social area by means of precise rules. The disjuncture between the sphere of necessity and the sphere of autonomy is an essential condition for the greatest possible expansion of the latter.

9. The Sphere of Necessity: The State

The sphere of necessity encompasses two types of heteronomous activity: that required for the social production of necessities, and that required for the functioning of society as a material system. The capitalist model of development is characterised by a simultaneous expansion of both types of activity. As commodity production has become concentrated into larger and larger units and the geographical, as well as the social and technical, division of labour has grown, so the functioning of the economic apparatus has required a very rapid development of the network of state services: transport, telecommunications, the collection and centralisation of information, the training (schooling) and maintenance (health care) of the labour force, taxation, police, to name the most obvious. In other words, work linked to the administration and reproduction of social relations has grown more rapidly than work directly linked to material production, and has become a precondition of its heightened efficacy.[1] The mechanisms of the productive apparatus require a substantial sub-structure of administration and public service (the state apparatus) and, through its mediation, tend to transform society into a system of externalised relations in which individuals are not the acting subjects but the acted-upon objects. Society is thus corroded to the benefit of the state, as are the range of political options, freedoms and powers to the benefit of technocratic imperatives.

Thus the reduction of the sphere of necessity cannot merely involve reducing the amount of work required for material production of the necessities of life. It also necessitates a reduction in all the external diseconomies and state-regulated activities

---

1. Economists describe the phenomenon as 'tertiarisation'.

needed by direct production. This can only be achieved if the productive apparatus itself, and the division of labour to which it gives rise, are in turn modified.

It has been well established that the technical concentration of production into large-scale units results in diseconomies and social costs which may far outweigh the apparent economies of scale.[2] These latter consist of a higher rate of return on fixed capital: the same amount (say £1,000,000) invested in one large unit is supposed to yield a higher volume of production and a larger mass of profits than if it had been invested in a number of small units. But this type of calculation abstracts from the social investment and social costs entailed by the concentration of capital: the construction of transportation systems to supply the factories with raw materials and carry away their output; the need to house the labour force and hence to urbanise new areas; a rise in municipal service and administration costs disproportionate to the expansion of the urban area; higher travel costs for the labour force etc.

In addition to these indirect social costs borne by the collectivity as a whole, there are also a number of 'invisible costs': a disproportionate increase in environmental pollution and degradation; an increase in ill-health among the population; the more rigid management and functioning of a large-scale unit of production which, because of its very high capital cost, calls for the most tightly controlled load factor and amortisation schedule. A large unit of production is likely to have to work day and night, thus increasing the physical and nervous strain for its workforce. It will have greater difficulty in adjusting production to qualitative or quantitative variations in consumer requirements, and will therefore seek to produce and maintain a constant or growing level of demand for its output. Hence demand is likely to be subordinated to supply, and the needs of the population to the technical and financial imperatives of capital. The result is a commercial strategy designed to produce consumers who match the product on offer, and to satisfy every conceivable need through the maximum sale of commodities. This, in turn, tends

---

2. See especially, J.-M. Chevalier, *L'Economie industrielle en question*, Paris, 1977 and A. Lovins, *Soft Energy Paths*, Harmondsworth, Penguin 1977.

to set the consumption of energy, raw materials, state-run services and public amenities at the maximum level.

In short, the quest for the lowest direct cost per unit of production and the highest return on capital leads to the highest level of indirect social costs. The total (direct and indirect) cost of centralised production is often higher than that involved in smaller and apparently less efficient units.

For all these reasons, a trend reversal has begun to manifest itself around the theme *Small is Beautiful*.[3] Only small- or medium-sized units of production can be subordinated to the needs of the population, controlled by it and brought into line with local goals and resources. They alone make it possible to aim for the lowest level of total costs and the most favourable working conditions and environmental effects. They alone lend themselves to workers' management and contribute to the autonomy of regional and local communities. Self-management and the withering away of the state are only possible in a social space in which small units are able to re-establish a direct relation, if not a unity, between producers and consumers, town and country and the spheres of work and non-work. In short, reduction of the sphere of heteronomy requires decentralisation and a certain level of local self-sufficiency.

How far is it possible to reduce the sphere of heteronomy or the sphere of the state? Is there not a threshold beyond which the transfer of the state's functions to the local community no longer yields increased autonomy? Is there an advantage — and if so, how much of an advantage — in abolishing the sphere of necessity as a *distinct sphere* which imposes *external* rules and obligations, in such a way that necessities are assumed and internalised by each community and each individual?

Every type of communal experiment has encountered these questions, and most of them have failed because they have been unable to answer them. Thus libertarian, communal or self-management theories always start from the implicit assumption that heteronomy (or external constraints and obligations) is the product not of physical laws governing the material field of individual actions, but *only* of the way in which such actions are

---

3. E.F. Schumacher, *Small is Beautiful*, London, Blond and Briggs 1973.

articulated in different types of social organisation and cooperation. They always assume that it *must* be possible to subsume and dissolve the sphere of heteronomy in its autonomous counterpart. They always imagine that the appearance of communities that are manageable on a human scale *must* make it possible to do without functions which can only be carried out by state agencies external to the local community. Hence it *must* be possible to eliminate those 'tools' (including public facilities and institutions) which, being too big for communal control and self-management on a human scale, imply a quasi-military hierarchy and division of labour: large factories and giant amenities such as motorways, dams, rail or telecommunications systems, centralised energy systems etc. Consequently it *must* be possible that production necessities should cease to exist as external constraints and obligations; that necessary labour should be devised and allocated so as to be indistinguishable from free, creative and fulfilling activity; and that it should be an opportunity for festivity and human communication. In short, necessary labour *must* be capable of arrangement in such a way that the ideal (ethical) goal of a freely chosen mode of cooperation and existence is realised in the production of life's necessities.

There is only one type of community that actually corresponds to such a unity of material necessity and ethical exigency: namely, the various monastic forms from the Cistercians and ashrams through the neo-buddhist or neo-muslim sects to the rural or artisanate 'communes'. The distinctive characteristic of such communities, however, is that necessary labour is not carried out because of its mere necessity or with a view to the realisation of its primary end. All activities and relations within a monastic-type community are mediated by their religious significance. Work is a particular form of prayer, or of communion with a transcendent order. Its primary aim is not to produce what is necessary but to allow God to be revealed within everyday life. Equally, the members of such communities do not have relations of direct reciprocity or horizontal communication with one another. In their relations of mediated reciprocity, the goal is not to communicate with, or give to, other individuals, but to cooperate with all in achieving communion with God.[4]

---

4. The same observations, as well as the following analysis, could be applied to

It is of no great importance whether the religious sentiment informing such relationships be Christian, pantheist, maoist, neo-buddhist or animist. What counts is the sanctification of daily activities, so that simple primary ends disappear behind the highly elaborate ritual of performance.

In communities of this type the unity of the spheres of necessity and freedom, heteronomy and autonomy, is achieved much more by symbolic insinuation than by the elimination of external necessities and constraints. These appear to be freely chosen only insofar as each individual member regards them as something other than they are: the most banal types of material production are seen as a form of spiritual exercise; and the necessity of their execution is regarded not as a chore undertaken because 'it's got to be done' but as a work of moral and religious mortification and self-abnegation.

In other words, the realm of necessity is not abolished but sublimated, and — in this sublimated form — it continues to govern every moment of communal life: timetables, strict rules and obligations, hierarchy and discipline, division of tasks, the duty of obedience, devotion and love.[5]

These are *inevitable* characteristics of a community in which

---

societies or communities without a history. There, activities required to maintain the life of the group or society are given the sublimated form of religious injunctions, while the manner of their accomplishment is codified into sacred rituals, so that what is eventually achieved is perceived as a reward bestowed by the gods for the faithful observance of duty towards them. It used to be customary to ascribe to 'prelogical mentality' this sublimation of laws and physical necessities into the demands of a transcendent (divine) figure and the resultant confusion between imperatives of a technical and a moral and religious nature.

5. Obviously there can be no place for couples and the exclusivity of love in these types of communities. Because they are based on a complete identification of the individual with the community, communities of the monastic type are forced to either repress or exclude any form of sexual relationship as something that cannot be mediated by the group, or to collectivise sexual life by prohibiting the formation of couples and encouraging group sexuality or the rotation of partners. In either case, the group represses the love of one person for another, insofar as it represents a threat or, worse, a negation of the cohesion and sovereignty of the community. On the repression of the singular love relations by revolutionary communities, see Kazimierz Brandys, 'Défense de Grenade' in *La mère des rois*, Paris, 1957 and Daniel Cohn-Bendit, *Le grand bazar*, Paris, Pierre Belfond 1976.

the necessities of communal life have to be assumed and internalised by each individual, since each individual is responsible for the survival and cohesion of the community as a whole. No questioning is allowed of the practical necessities and constraints of communal life. For since these necessities are not regulated by an institution distinct from the community itself, opposition would be directed against the community in question and lead to expulsion of the infractor. Thus the cohesion of the community is based upon the internalisation of practical constraints as ethical duties, and the prohibition of revolt or disobedience on pain of exclusion, dishonour or the withdrawal of love. Individual goals and collective duties, personal life and group interest are merged into one, so that the love of *each* member of the community for *all* the others (and not for *each* other) becomes the prime *duty*. It is invoked in recognition of the fact that the united community — personified in the Mother or Father Superior, Big Brother or Beloved Leader — has become the source of each individual member's life and identity. Thus an apparent abolition of external constraints is achieved only by transforming them into internal obligations. The constraints and sanctions of the law are abolished only to give way to the most tyrannical law: the *duty to love*.

In all of its aspects, the community of work and life merely reproduces the primal group that lies at the core of every communal experiment — namely, the family as it existed when the household was fundamentally a productive unit assuming the subsistence of its members. If the state — or the apparatus of the law — is understood as a *distinct locus* in which the necessities of production and communal life are embodied in external laws and obligations, then any society or micro-society that abolishes the state thereby loses all capacity to challenge the material necessities of its own functioning. Such societies find themselves inexorably bound to the 'duty to love'. Their members will be obliged, through love, to obey a spiritual father or communal leader whose genius-like omniscience, enlightened will, innate wisdom and radiant generosity make him or her an indisputable authority. Through figures such as these, the sphere of necessity is personified and sublimated into a subjective will. Material constraints are translated into ethical duties. The objectivity of the law and practical necessity is abolished in favour of personal authority, charismatic power and tyranny.

The specific characteristic of such figures — whether a spiritual father, the head of a productive commune, a charismatic leader or a ('benevolent') tyrant — is their capacity to demand and obtain *submission to necessity as a submission to their own person*. The leader enunciates the law, which is also duty. Through the leader's mediation what has to be done in the interests of group life and survival becomes something expected of each individual, not as the realisation of some technical requirement ('because it's needed'), but rather as a recognition of the leader's authority, an act of allegiance, an expression of love for her or his person. Hagiographies of Hitler or Stalin are unequivocal on this point. The leader is someone who, through (parental) love for the community, takes its operational necessities upon himself or herself and transforms them into personal orders and obligations; and ensures that its members are prepared, as a mark of their love for him or her, to undertake things that they would scarely contemplate doing for themselves. It is the leader who defines and allocates tasks, praise and blame, rewards and punishment. In the leader's person the moral law and physical laws, ethical obligations and material necessities are joined so that it becomes impossible to oppose the one without opposing the other. All criticism becomes subversion, all debate a refusal to obey or, in micro-societies, a refusal to love.

A disjuncture between the sphere of necessity and the area of autonomy, an objectification of the operational necessities of communal life in the form of laws, prohibitions and obligations, the existence of a system of law distinct from mere usage and of a state distinct from society — these are the very preconditions of a sphere in which autonomous individuals may freely cooperate for their own ends. Only a dissociation of the spheres of heteronomy and autonomy makes it possible to confine objective necessities and obligations to a clearly circumscribed area, and thus to open up a space for autonomy entirely free of their imperatives.

This is as true of large societies as of micro-societies based on communal life and production. The only type of 'commune' that manages to survive is one in which the sphere of necessity (that is, the mass of necessary work and obligations) has been clearly defined, codified and programmed.[6] This objective definition of what is necessariiy required of each individual is the only means of separating the time allocated to necessary labour from that available for freely chosen activities. Only such a distinction allows everyone to know when their relations with others are objectively determined by material necessity (the need to collect the rubbish, oil machines, keep to the railway timetable, pick the fruit before the frost etc.) and when they derive from an autonomous subjective choice. Only the latter category of relations is the province of moral judgement and ethics, since morality knows no necessity and necessity no morality. The objectification of a set of obligations external to each individual yet common to them all is the only means of protecting the members of the community from the personal power of a leader, with all its associated emotional blackmail and arbitrary behaviour.[7]

The existence of a state separate from civil society, able both to codify objective necessities in the form of law and to assure its implementation, is thus the essential prerequisite to the autonomy of civil society and the emergence of an area outside the sphere of heteronomy in which a variety of modes of production, modes of life and forms of cooperation can be experimented with according to individual desires. As the site at which the law is formulated and the material imperatives of the social system are translated into universally applicable objective rules known to everyone, the state serves to free civil society and its individual members from tasks which they could only undertake at the price of impairing both individual and social relations. Thus the existence of money and prices makes it possible to avoid the haggling and mutual suspicion that go along with

6. This happen's most particularly on kibbutzim.
7. Those who have frequented the community of intellectual research and experiment constituted by the CIDOC at Cuernavaca, have found (with astonishment in the case of French leftists) that individual or collective autonomy unfolded within a framework of rules to which no exceptions were permitted. These rules particularly concerned the fees, timetable, and the inviolability of certain areas. Illich's refusal to allow anyone to be exempted from these rules was a refusal to allow his personal power to be substituted for the codified, impersonal objectivity of the procedures required for the working of the CIDOC.

barter and the lack of any system of equivalences.[8] Similarly, the existence of a police (whose functions need not be carried out as a full-time career) makes it unnecessary for each individual to internalise a whole system of law and order. The existence of a highway code makes it unnecessary to negotiate with other road users at every intersection. The basic function of legal rules is to define forms of conduct which, because they are notoriously predetermined, cannot be imputed personally to those carrying them out. Everyone is well aware of the impersonal, anonymous nature of such conduct and its dependence on externally defined laws, and therefore follows them without claiming personal responsibility or holding others responsible. By observing such predefined patterns, individuals *function* socially as component parts of a social system which determines their conduct.[9] The act of purchasing and paying for something in a shop is, for example, an anonymous action that in no way involves buyer and seller in personal relations.

All codification and regulation of behaviour results in the replacement of reciprocal human relations by non-relations or non-human relations in which individuals function as the component parts of a pre-set mechanism. Non-relations such as these stem from the inertial requirements of society as a machine — as a trivial system, to use von Foerster's words — as a set of factories, administrations, transport and telecommunications networks etc. Here relations between individuals are mediated by relations between things, or are subordinated and even reduced to relations between things. They are in essence trivial, heteronomous relations.

Only trivialisation of relations regulating the sphere of necessity can lead to the abolition of the 'struggle for life', the

---

8. To use the phrase invented by Everett Reimer which Illich loves to cite, 'Money is the cheapest currency.'
9. Politeness is the archetype of this form of behaviour. Polite conduct is a refusal to establish a personal relationship by adhering to the rules of etiquette. Thus individuals make no pretence to originality and merely inhabit the role prescribed for them by circumstances. Politeness enables individuals to enter into a relationship without conflict insofar as they inhabit a series of social *personae*, without giving anything of themselves or committing themselves in any way.

struggle between individuals and groups to secure life's necessities and/or to hoard essential goods. In this sense, socially planned production of what is needed by everyone is a basic prerequisite for the pacification of social relations and the emergence of autonomous human relations. This was seen by Marx. The existence of a centrally planned sector of production and distribution, able both to provide the necessities of life for everyone and to define the amount of socially necessary labour required from each individual in order to be free of need, makes the sphere of necessity a distinct and clearly circumscribed area in which trivialised technical behaviour is the norm. The area of complete autonomy lies outside this area.

Only rigorous delimitation of this centrally planned, trivialised sphere makes it possible to establish a sphere of the fullest autonomy, in which individuals are free to associate according to their desires in order to create what is beyond necessity. If social planning is extended to all activities and transactions, the sphere of autonomy is negated and asphyxiated. But if, through the absence of centralised social planning, production and distribution are left to follow the interests of those in possession of the means of production and distribution, then inequality and the fear of scarcity ensure that the struggle for both necessities and non-necessities continues to mark social relations. Society continues to be divided into an entirely dependent class and a class whose control of the means of production and exchange guarantees its domination of the entire society.

Failure to trivialise the sphere of necessity through regionally and locally inflected central planning does not therefore imply an increase of autonomy, but an increase of domination and heteronomy. Inversely, failure to limit social trivialisation to the sphere of necessity replaces the domination of a class with the general domination of an apparatus. This is why economic liberalism gives rise to demands for state control, and why state control provokes demands for liberalisation. The point, however, is not to choose one or the other; but to define the field in which both can be cogently put into effect. The field of liberalism cannot comprise socially necessary activities; nor can the field of social trivialisation embrace socially non-necessary activity. The creation of 'superfluities' and the production of necessities cannot be subject to the same social rules.

The problem facing a 'post-industrial socialism' is therefore the abolition not of the state but of domination. Law and domination, the state apparatus and the apparatus of domination need to be dissociated from one another. Until now, however, they have always been confused.[10] The state structures are not, in fact, the source of every type of domination, nor its most fundamental cause. They are called into being by social relations of domination (the domination of one class over society as a whole) which they themselves extend and consolidate by adding their distinctive domination effects. The domination of society by the state is as much a result as a precondition of its domination by technical and economic concentrations of capital. The large capitalist systems (factories and warehouses, office blocks and big stores etc.) create a demand for public services, and that in turn gives rise to giant state apparatuses whose own mechanisms reinforce the power of capitalist domination. Society is thus crushed under the weight of administrative machines with their own physical laws and inert imperatives. In that way, the sphere of heteronomy comes to encompass social life as a whole.

The reduction of this sphere cannot just be a matter of reducing the state's sphere of influence. The highest priority cannot be accorded to denationalisation, the transfer of public services to the private sector, financial cutbacks, and so on. If the sphere of heteronomy is to be reduced together with the state and its agencies, there must be a simultaneous reduction in every other instrument or apparatus which, by virtue of its size, has become a means of domination. The state, however, remains the indispensable tool of this double reduction: it alone is capable of protecting society against the domination of giant tools; it alone is capable of ensuring that the means of producing necessities are not monopolised by a social class for the purposes of domination. Its capacity for coordination and centralised regulation makes it the sole agency able to reduce socially necessary labour time to a minimum. It is, finally, the only agency able to reduce its own power and influence in favour of an enlarged sphere of autonomy.

10. See part 3, chapter 2 above.

It goes without saying that the state will do none of that on its own initiative. It is a tool indispensable for coordination and regulation, for the limitation of other tools, and for the trivialisation of socially necessary tasks and behaviour. But it will only produce these results if it is organised *with these results in mind* by a society able to use it both to change itself and to serve its own ends. The transformation of the state is *one* prerequisite for the transformation of society. It is not, however, the priority to which all other changes should be subordinated. The state can only cease to be an apparatus of domination over society and become an instrument enabling society to exercise power over itself with a view to its own restructuring, if society is already permeated by social struggles that open up areas of autonomy keeping both the dominant class and the power of the state apparatus in check. The establishment of new types of social relations, new ways of producing, associating, working and consuming is the fundamental precondition of any political transformation. The dynamic of social struggles is the lever by which society can act upon itself and establish a range of freedoms, a new state and a new system of law.

Only the movement itself, through its own practice, can create and extend the sphere of autonomy in which new freedoms will be born. The movement cannot, however, just through its own practice, found a new state and legal system. It can tear apart and recast the fabric of the old system of social relations — and it alone is capable of doing so. But it does not have the vocation or the means to reorganise society and to ensure that the system materially functions in such a way that the resultant sphere of heteronomy occupies the least possible space.

Unless a number of tasks are fulfilled, the goals of the movement cannot find practical expression at the level of society as a whole, nor result in the constant restructuring of social organisation. These tasks are: to delimit and codify the sphere of necessity, and hence to define the attributes of the state; to draw up the guidelines and instruments of a central planning system; and to weigh up the various priorities and constraints attaching to otherwise equivalent choices.

These tasks can be neither entrusted to the state nor undertaken by the movement. They represent the specific domain of **politics. Politics** is the site of tension and always conflictual mediation between, on the one hand, the enlargement of the sphere of autonomy impelled by the demands of the movement flowing through civil society and, on the other hand, the state-regulated necessities arising from the workings of society as a material system. Politics is the specific site at which society becomes conscious of its own production as a complex process and seeks both to master the results of that process and to bring its constraints under control.

This is why the function of the political cannot be exercised unless it is distinct from both the state and the aspirations rising from civil society. It can only function as the site of mediation, reflection and trade-off between the demands for autonomy and the imperatives of technicity, between subjectivity and objective constraints, if it is successful in avoiding identification with either of the two poles between which it is located. The political should, on the contrary, be the area of maximum tension, where the debate over ends — their conditions of possibility and the paths that lead to them — is always open and explicit.

Thus the essential purpose of politics is not the exercise of power. On the contrary, its function is to delimit, orient and codify the actions of government, to designate the ends and means they should use, and to ensure that they do not stray from their mission. Any confusion between politics and power, or between political struggle and the struggle for power (that is, for the right to run the state), signifies the death of politics. For instead of being the mediation between the movement actively at work within civil society and the management of society as a system, politics then becomes the site of one-way mediation, merely transmitting the technical requirements of state management to civil society and channelling any flicker of a movement into the paths already opened by the state.

In this case, political parties, whether in opposition or in government, become the transmission belts of the state power they exercise or hope to exercise. Instead of questioning the technical necessities with aspirations to autonomy — and vice versa — they combat, repress or absorb and neutralise autonomous movements complicating or threatening to complicate the exercise of state power. In doing so, however, they dig their own graves. For politics can only exist as a distinct space, and a political party as a distinct force, if society is permeated by autonomous movements, aspirations, struggles, desires and oppositions which form a barrier to total state management and continually appropriate new areas of autonomy. If parties cut themselves off from autonomous movements, they become no more than electoral machines singing the praises of their respective candidates for technocratic power — that is, for state management of the sphere of necessity.[11]

Once abandoned by political parties, the site of the political tends to move elsewhere. Throughout the capitalist West we can see a process similar to that which has already occurred in the United States. There, fundamental debates over the production and the transformation of society have shifted to clubs, churches, universities, associations and movements whose aim is not to exercise state power over society, but to extricate the latter from the former in order to enlarge the area of autonomy and self-determination, which is also the sphere of ethical relations.

Just as the belief in 'progress' through scientific, technological and industrial development has died away, so too has the positivist outlook which equates the state with the supreme good and politics with religion or even morality. We know now that there is no 'good' government, 'good' state or 'good' form of power, and that society can never be 'good' in its own organisation but only by virtue of the space for self-organisation, autonomy, cooperation and voluntary exchange which that organisation offers to individuals.

The beginning of wisdom lies in the recognition that there are contradictions whose permanent tension has to be lived and which one should never try to resolve; that reality is made up of distinct levels which have to be acknowledged in their specificity and never reduced to an 'average'; that necessity knows no morality and morality no necessity; that the physical laws governing the workings of systems can never be translated into ethical rules, nor ethical rules into physical laws; that there is no system able to free us despite ourselves or make us happy or 'moral' behind our backs. For happiness, like morality, always consists

---

11. This is one of the main arguments put forward by Alain Touraine, especially in *Mort d'une gauche*, Paris, Galilée 1979, and by Pierre Rosanvallon and Patrick Viveret in *Pour une nouvelle culture politique*, Paris, Editions du Seuil 1977.

in being able to realise freely chosen ends and to take as ends the actions that one realises.

Politics is not morality, just as morality is not politics. Politics is the site at which moral exigencies confront external necessities. This confrontation will last for as long as, in Hegel's phrase, consciousness does not encounter the world 'as a garden laid out for its benefit'. Only the permanence and openness of this confrontation can ensure that the sphere of necessity is as small and the sphere of autonomy as large as possible.

Destructive Growth and Productive Shrinking

What do we need? What do we desire? What do we lack in order to fulfil ourselves, to communicate with others, to lead more relaxed lives and establish more loving relations? Economic forecasting and political economy in general have nothing to offer here. Concerned as they are simply to keep the machines turning over, to keep capital circulating, or to maintain a certain level of employment, they manufacture the needs which correspond at any given moment to the requirements of the machinery of production and circulation. Deliberately and systematically, they supply us with new wants and new scarcities, new types of luxury and new senses of poverty, in conformity with capital's need for profitability and growth. Capital has at its service a number of strategists who are capable of manipulating our most intimate desires in order to impose their products upon us by means of the symbols with which they are charged.

Twenty years ago, one such strategist spilled the beans with considerable candour. He was Stanley Resor, president of J. Walter Thompson, one of the biggest advertising agencies in the USA. He said:

> When income goes up, the most important thing is to create new needs. If you ask people 'Do you know that your standard of living will go up by 50% in ten years?', they haven't got the faintest idea what that means. They don't realise that they need a second car unless they are carefully reminded. The need has to be created in their minds. They have to be brought to realise all the advantages of having a second car. I see advertising as an educational, activating force capable of producing the changes in demand which we need. By educating people into higher living standards, it ensures

that consumption will rise to a level justified by our productivity and resources.[1]

That is quite clear: consumption is subordinated to production. It must supply the outlets required by production, and express needs corresponding to the output which technological change makes most profitable at any given moment. All this is indispensable if society is to perpetuate itself, if its hierarchical inequalities are to be reproduced and its mechanisms of domination are to remain intact.

The consumer forecasts which guide economic activity are always based on the hypothesis that there will be no major change in society, life-styles or the forms of production and consumption. The rich and the poor will always be there, just as there will always be people who command and people who obey, or crowded underground stations and half-empty Concordes. We will always be in a hurry and never have sufficient time or inclination for autonomous activities. We will never have any desire or capacity to think about our needs, to debate the best means of satisfying them, and to choose corresponding collective options through a sovereign act.

The idea that production and consumption can be decided on the basis of needs is, by implication, politically subversive. It suggests that producers and consumers could meet, discuss matters and make sovereign decisions. It presupposes the abolition of the monopoly exercised by capital and/or the state over decisions concerning investment, production and innovation. It presupposes a consensus about the nature and level of consumption to which everyone should be entitled, and hence about the limits that should not be crossed.[2] Finally, it presupposes a form

---

1. Cited in A. Gorz, *La morale de l'histoire*, Paris, Editions du Seuil 1959.
2. Those who think that it would be impossible to establish a consensus over the limits and level of consumption will find the following example in R.G. Schwartzenberg, *Sociologie politique*, Paris, Monchrétien 1977:

> According to a poll carried out by the Norwegian Government Food and Health Agency in 1975, 76 percent of the respondents were dissatisfied. They felt that the standard of living of their country was '*too high*'. A substantial majority would have preferred 'a calm, simple life, with just what was needed'. They would have liked 'income and careerism to be limited'.

of economic management designed to satisfy a maximum of needs with the greatest possible efficiency, (that is to say, with the minimum of labour, capital and natural resources, the minimum of commodity production).

Now, such goals constitute a radical negation of the logic of capitalism. The option of maximum efficiency and minimum waste is so foreign to the rationality of the system that macroeconomic theory does not even possess the tools with which to grasp it. Gains realised through more efficient management appear as *losses* in the national statistics: a decline in GNP and in the volume of goods and services at the disposal of the population.

This serves to indicate the level of distortion built into official methods of accounting and forecasting. They present any growth in output and purchasing as a rise in national wealth, even if it includes the growing quantity of throw-away packaging, gadgets and metal thrown on the refuse-tips, paper burnt along with rubbish, non-repairable household goods; it even includes artificial limbs and medical care required by victims of industrial or road accidents. Destruction officially appears as a source of wealth since the replacement of everything broken, thrown out or lost gives rise to new production, sales, monetary flows and profits. The more quickly things are broken, worn out, made obsolete or thrown away, the larger the GNP will be and the wealthier the national statistics will say we are. Even illness and physical injury are presented as sources of wealth, for they swell the consumption of drugs and health-care facilities.

But what if the opposite were the case? If good health made it possible to reduce medical expenditure, if the things we use were to last half a life-time without becoming obsolete or worn out, if they could be repaired or even adapted without recourse to specialised paid services, then GNP would of course decline. We would work fewer hours, consume less and have fewer needs.

How does one replace an economic system based on the quest for maximum waste with a system based on the quest for minimum waste? The question is over a century old. It amounts to asking how an economy in which production is subordinated to capital's need for profits may be replaced by an economy (originally known as socialism) in which production is subordinated to needs (and in which needs are freely determined by people themselves in the light of the means and costs of their possible satisfaction). Only a mode of production divested of the drive to accumulate and expand can invest today in order to save tomorrow — that is to say, in order to satisfy every type of need with a *smaller* volume of *more durable* products upon which profits, as now understood, will also be lower. Whereas the impossible chimera of perpetual growth is experienced as crisis and falling living standards, shrinking social production will, under 'post-industrial socialism', result from a conscious decision to do more and live better with less. This is the essence of its superiority over capitalism.

In fact, the term 'post-industrial socialism' is inappropriate here. Marxist terminology would have us refer straightforwardly to 'communism', meaning that stage in which the 'fullest development of the productive forces' has been realised and where the principal task is no longer to maximise production or assure full employment, but to achieve a different organisation of the economy so that a full day's work is no longer a precondition for the right to a full income. To put it another way, it is a society in which everyone is entitled to the satisfaction of his or her needs in return for an amount of socially necessary labour occupying only a small fraction of a lifetime.

We have almost reached that stage. The complete satisfaction of every need through a small amount of labour is now impeded not by insufficient development of the means of production, but rather by their overdevelopment. The system has not been able to grow and reproduce itself by accelerating the destruction as well as the production of commodities, by organising new scarcities as the mass of wealth has increased, by devaluing wealth when it threatens to become available to all, by perpetuating poverty alongside privilege, and frustration alongside opulence.

The development of the productive forces within the framework of capitalism will never lead to the threshold of communism. For the very nature of its products, technology and relations of production precludes any lasting and equitable satisfaction of needs, as well as any stabilisation of social production at a commonly acceptable level of *sufficiency*. The very idea that there might one day be *enough* for all and that the quest for 'more' and 'better' might give way to extra-economic, non-market goals and values is alien to capitalist society. It is, however, essential to communism. And communism can take shape as the positive negation of the existing system only if the ideas of self-limitation, stabilisation, equity and non-monetary exchange are given practical illustration — if, in other words, it is practically demonstrated not only that it is possible to live better by working differently and consuming less, but that voluntary, collective limitation of the sphere of necessity is the way, and the only way, to guarantee an extension of the sphere of autonomy.

Hence the importance of 'social experiments' with new ways of living together, consuming, producing and cooperating. Hence also the importance of alternative technologies which make it possible to do more, better and with less, while at the same time increasing the autonomy of individuals and local communities.

The fact that these technologies have mainly been developed by militant groups as indispensable tools for a different model of society does not mean, however, that they can achieve their objectives on the margin of politics, or that they prefigure a society in which the state will have been abolished through the transfer of all its functions to self-governing communities. If the time spent by individuals in producing necessities is to be reduced to a minimum, together with their dependence on the vagaries of local circumstance, then the socialisation of the production of necessities and centralised regulation of distribution and exchange will remain essential. The sphere of necessity, and with it the amount of time involved in socially necessary labour, can only be reduced to a minimum by the most efficient coordination and regulation of stocks and flows or, in other words, by finely geared planning. If each individual is to be guaranteed a lifelong social income in return for 20,000 hours of socially useful work — supplied in any number of fractions, continuously or discontinuously, in one or several sectors of activity — then this can only be achieved by means of a centralised mechanism of regulation and adjustment: in other words, a state.

The alternative to the present system is therefore neither a return to household economy and village autarky, nor total planning and socialisation of every activity. Instead, it consists in reducing what has necessarily to be done, whether enjoyable or not, to a minimum of each person's lifetime, and in extending as far as possible collective and/or individual autonomous activity seen as an end in itself.

It is essential to reject both the assumption of complete state responsibility for the individual, and the internalisation by each individual of responsibility for the necessities intrinsic to the operation of society as a material system. Identification of the individual with the state, and of the requirements of the state with individual happiness, are the two faces of totalitarianism.

As Marx indicated at the end of volume 3 of *Capital*, the sphere of necessity cannot be merged with the sphere of autonomy. This is why an extension of the latter presupposes a clear delimitation and codification of the former. These are in essence political tasks. Politics is not about the exercise of power; its function is to equip the state with the tasks and forms of management best able to reduce the sphere of heteronomy and enlarge the sphere of autonomy.

But politics has no purchase or specific reality unless society itself is permeated by movements of social struggle that seek to capture broader spaces of autonomy from capitalist and state domination. By rejecting movements of struggle, or by subordinating them to their present or future exercise of state power, political parties have entered into decline. Out of an anxiety to preserve their own monopoly, they now try to prevent the rebirth of politics in different forms and on different ground. As a result, they are in even greater disrepute. There can be no cause for rejoicing in their suicide. The death of politics heralds the birth of the total state.

Towards a Policy of Time

The robot revolution

During the past ten years, a million jobs (or one job in six) have been eliminated in French industry. Yet the process of automation has only just begun. More than any of the great transformations of the past, it is a technological revolution affecting the very bases of the social order established over the last 150 years. The respective values of work, time and money are being called into question.

All the economics textbooks still explain that technical progress is a costly affair, involving the replacement of human labour by machines, or wages by capital. The more efficient the machinery, it is said, the more costly it is likely to be. Only the most powerful corporations can afford the most efficient machines.

But what has previously been true is no longer the case. Micro-electronics (of which robots are one applied example) has the previously unheard-of characteristic of making it possible to economise not just on human labour, but on *labour and capital at the same time*. They allow you, if you are an employer, to replace nine-tenths of your workforce with machines — while paying less for these ultra-efficient machines than for the ones you used previously. Here are two typical examples.

Suppose you have a large finance department with a pool of 120 typists, each using a typewriter in a huge work area. You can now replace them with eight secretaries, working in a comfortable office with eight word-processors. Those eight machines will cost you much less than 120 ordinary typewriters. You will also save the cost of 112 people's wages. Your fixed costs will fall and your middle management will have much more time. Instead of dictating letters, they will merely indicate the code numbers corresponding to whole paragraphs stored in the word-processor.

A second example: You employ two engineers and 15 drafters in a precision metalwork foundry. Their job is to design the complicated parts from which moulds will be taken. If you buy a plotter, a computerised machine that does the designing, you will be able to employ a single person (an engineer) instead of 17.

In the light of these examples, there is no need to ask why investment has fallen and profits risen in almost every industrialised country in recent years. (Since 1973 profits in the French private sector have risen by 23 per cent; investment has fallen by 3 per cent.) The reason is self-evident: automation has made it possible to produce a growing quantity of goods and services with less and less capital. And this is only the beginning. In five to ten years' time, much more efficient robots will be mass-produced *by robots* at knock-down prices.

So, if you are an employer, you will decide that you have to wait. In a few years' time, you will be able to acquire for much less money even more efficient machines than those you forego buying today.

This is why it is pointless to expect a spontaneous revival of economic growth in the next few years. All that can be achieved is a sort of voluntarist growth, stimulated by state-financed investment, regardless of short-term profitability or competitiveness, in such areas as public facilities, housing, research, energy conservation, mineral prospecting, protection of the environment — or armaments.

But will there not be a revival in five or ten years' time? Will the race to automate industries, offices and services not result in an investment boom, a fall in unemployment and a new period of growth comparable to the one that began some 35 years ago? The nature of the changes underway provides the answer to such questions.

According to the president of General Motors, the assembly-line will have disappeared from American automobile factories by 1988. Their stock of machines will be 90 per cent computer controlled, and 50 per cent of their unskilled workforce will have gone. The president of the world's largest automobile corporation is unwilling to go into more detail about the consequences of this re-equipment programme, but some of his Japanese counterparts have been less discreet. One of them — the managing director of Fujitsu Fanuc — gave European journalists a guided tour of a factory producing the robots that will be used by the group's subsidiaries. A hundred workers, working in three shifts, are at present producing 100 robots a month. In fact they are only involved in the final assembly, since everything else in the factory has been automated. The basic materials are automatically loaded onto carriages that make their own way to the appropriate unit and supply the machine tool in question. This has been programmed to machine the parts in a memorised sequence of actions. It can be re-programmed from a distance *in a few minutes* to make various series of different parts. With conventional machine tools, the same procedures would take from eight to fifteen hours.

These 100 workers at Fujitsu Fanuc produce an output that would require 500 workers in a traditional factory. And this is only the beginning. In 1986 Fujitsu Fanuc will employ 200 people for an output that would have required 2,800 workers a few years ago.

Similar plans exist at Hitachi. One of its directors has stated: 'By 1986 we expect to have eliminated workers from the shop floor. The only people working in our factories will be a few maintenance technicians and administrative staff.'

These are second-generation robots — able not only to touch, feel and grip (as the first generation could do) but also to see, operate and monitor other fixed robots, repairing them if necessary and controlling the quality of finished parts. At the beginning of the next decade, the third generation will make its appearance in factories and offices. It will be able to understand and execute verbal instructions.

Manufacturers of robots and computerised systems can look forward to an immense market. The figures speak for themselves: in 1977 robot production amounted to 1,700 units; in 1978 the output of 32,000 units exceeded the total number already in service. In 1985 production will amount to over 100,000 units.

Robot production is growing at the rate of 33 per cent a year and the cost of a unit with the same performance is falling at an annual rate of 35 per cent. In 1974 a robot cost five to eight times as much as the non-computerised equipment needed for the same output. At present a robot sells for just £10,000 or so, covering its costs within less than a year.

Table 1: *Number of Industrial Robots 1980*

Japan	8,500
USA	3,255
Italy	800
Sweden	600
West Germany	350
Great Britain	185
France	180
Holland	170

This figure calls for some comment. The majority of politicians and economists continue to believe that,

> in order to create a single job it is necessary to invest some £10,000 for an unskilled job and as much as a £100,000 in sophisticated and complex plant. More than £10 billion a year would be needed to create 300,000 jobs a year. (*Le Monde* 5 September 1981)

The misunderstanding could not be more complete. These days, when £10,000 is invested, at least one job, and often two or three, are *eliminated* rather than created, as robots are used instead of people. A robot costing £10,000 makes it possible to save more than this sum in wages in under a year. In other words, the meaning of investment is changing completely. As Charles Levinson, the leader of the International Chemicals Federation (ICF), said over ten years ago, investment is no longer creating but destroying jobs. In more or less every type of industrial or office work, progress consists in producing more by working less.

Whatever the mythology, this is even true of Japan. Despite the sustained growth of the Japanese national product, automation eliminated over a million jobs there between 1973 and 1978. In the Datsun company, where the assembly of 1300 cars a day now requires only 67 workers, it is estimated that each worker employed in the production of robots eliminates five shop-floor jobs a year. The more jobs are created in automation, the more rapidly they will disappear in other sectors.

Already the automation of telephone exchanges has led to the disappearance of switchboard operators. In the post office, automation has reduced to three the number of employees required to sort and cancel 27,600 letters an hour. At Citroën, only

551 workers were taken on as replacements for those who left in 1980, as against 7754 in 1977. In the German office equipment and computer industry, the workforce fell by 27.5 per cent in seven years (1970-77), while output rose 48.9 per cent. During the same period, ATT in the United States reduced its workforce by half. Philips forecasts the elimination of half its 380,000 jobs between now and 1990, despite a projected rise in output of 3 per cent a year.

The End of the Unskilled Worker?

A survey carried out by researchers from the University of Michigan and the Society of Manufacturing Engineers predicts that by 1990 the major centres of production in the USA will run on a 32-hour week (or four eight-hour days).

Changes in the nature, duration and allocation of work will be negotiated with the workforce in the following stages:
● from 1980 a new hierarchy of skills, ever more centred on the creation, realisation and maintenance of automated equipment, will come into being;
● by 1985 20 per cent of the workers currently employed in assembly will have been replaced by automated systems;
● by 1987 20 per cent of industrial jobs will be redesigned and 15 per cent of assembly systems automated;
● by 1988 50 per cent of the labour force employed in assembling small components will have been replaced.

The process will continue to accelerate. According to a study presented by the Stanford Research Institute to the United Auto Workers (UAW) in March 1979, 80 per cent of manual work will have been automated by the year 2000 which, at present working hours, would amount to the elimination of 20 million manual jobs from the present total of 25 million.

Source: Joël Le Quément, 'Les Robots, enjeux économiques et sociaux', La Documentation Française 1981, p.196.

In no country, as far as I am aware, has anyone yet published a study or comprehensive investigation of the likely effects of automation on industrial employment. The bosses have generally kept to themselves the fragmentary information at their disposal. The fear of giving ammunition to the unions has overridden the desire to know and control the future. There is, however, a substantial study of the future of office work. It was carried out by Siemens for its own purposes, and was to have remained confidential. As the firm that dominates German electrical and office machinery, Siemens wanted to know what the market for automated office equipment would be. It therefore made a survey of firms representative of their branch of the economy, whatever their size, employing a total of 2.7 million office workers. It found that 7-900,000 of these jobs are susceptible to automation before 1990. By extrapolating, Siemens concluded that 72 per cent of the jobs in the public services could be 'formalised' (i.e. codified and standardised as a first step to full computerisation) and 28 per cent automated by the end of this decade.

In the retail sector, 25 per cent of jobs could be eliminated by introducing electronic tills linked to a central memory bank able to automatically control stocks, make up order forms and draw up balances and inventories.

Siemens did not estimate how many jobs might be eliminated. That was not its purpose. But Mike Cooley, a British trade unionist and computer expert, has calculated that 3.9 million office jobs could disappear in Britain over the next ten years. With the combination of large and small computers, word-processors, plotters, electronic money, video communicators and the like, automation promises to make itself felt even more rapidly in the tertiary (retail and service) sector than in industry. Already it is estimated that 20-30 per cent of the staff of French banks and insurance companies (including the social security system) are redundant and have not been dismissed only for political reasons.

Thus it is no longer possible to count on the tertiary sector to compensate for the elimination of jobs in industry. On the contrary, as Jacques Attali has argued most convincingly, past excessive growth of the tertiary sector is one cause of the present crisis. (See his *Les Trois Mondes*, Paris 1981.) The tertiary sector accounted for three-quarters of the 3.7 million jobs created in France between 1962 and 1975. The banks and insurance companies in particular doubled the number of their employees during this period. Between 1974 and 1980, moreover, while 622,000 jobs were eliminated in French industry, twice as many were created in the tertiary sector. At present it employs 50 per cent more wage earners than industry.

Attali is not alone in pointing to the explosion of 'organisation costs' involved in this process. The weight of these costs, bound up with the huge size and complexity of the administrative

apparatus, has become a physical as well as an economic
obstacle to the smooth working of society. But by 'organisation
costs' Attali means more than the costs of the gigantic
mechanisms of coordination, decision-making, and the gather-
ing and passing on of information. Large-scale industry, he
writes, also requires the wide-ranging, omnipresent services of
education, research etc. to 'produce the demand' corresponding
to supply; to produce the consumers the industrial system needs
for its products. According to Attali, the present crisis will be
overcome through a technological transformation which raises
efficiency and drastically reduces the costs of 'organisational'
activity. This is, indeed, the specific feature of the revolution in-
augurated by micro-electronics. The new technology revolu-
tionises the means of producing non-material goods even more
than material goods.

This is why a reduction of work time is on the agenda in the
tertiary sector at least as much as in industry. In Sweden,
Finland, Britain and Italy, it is precisely the office workers who
first obtained a 36-hour week. APEX, one of the main British
white-collar unions, now has the aim of enforcing a 30-hour,
four-day week over the next five or six years. Already the union,
led by Roy Grantham, has signed path-breaking agreements
with major firms such as Plessey, Lucas and ICL providing for
an annual reduction of an hour a week to 28 or 30 hours —
without any loss of earnings, of course. Negotiations are also
underway with some 50 large engineering firms.

As Grantham sees it, this shortening of the working week as
productivity rises is the only way to maintain security of employment during the present phase of technological transformation.

Different solutions may however be devised according to the
particular situation and demands of the wage earners. Three
American examples indicate the varying dimensions of a policy
that links job security to the amount of time spent working.

In 1970 the United Auto Workers union (UAW) won a reduction not only in the working week but also in the length of the
working *life*. Its agreement with the employers imposed retirement not at 60 or 55, but after 30 years' employment. Its campaign had been fought under the slogan 'Thirty and Out!'

The steelworkers' union has waged a struggle for 'employment for life' and 'a wage for life' which has had some success.

Its draft collective agreement stipulates that, whatever the circumstances, its workers should never be paid for less than a 30-hour week, even if they only work 20 hours or are temporarily laid off. Conjunctural fluctuations in the size of the work force would thus be ruled out.

This is precisely what the New York dockers achieved in October 1976. They are now guaranteed an annual basic wage of $16,000, even if they only work a dozen weeks in the year. In these latter two agreements, guarantees of job security essentially entail a guaranteed income, irrespective of the number of hours worked.

In 'free-market' societies however agreements of this kind cannot be generalised. If they are unable to dismiss workers or cut wage bills, the bosses will protect themselves by taking on the barest minimum of permanently employed workers. Any work that can be subcontracted will then be entrusted to 'outside agencies' employing a temporary, floating work force without any rights or protection. This has happened particularly in Japan and the USA. Full-time workers there enjoy guaranteed employment and income but make up only a minority of the workforce: the remainder are subject to dismissal and unbridled exploitation.

In France this division between permanent and unprotected wage earners exists even within the nationalised sector (especially the national railways and Paris métro) as well as in the public services (schools, hospitals, the post office etc.), where a mass of short-term workers liable to dismissal without notice and a large number of 'temporaries' supplied by private agencies are employed alongside protected and tenured employees.

Thus, however powerful they are, and however well they protect their members, trade unions are not by themselves able to provide the population as a whole with the right to a job, shorter working hours and a guaranteed income for life. State action is also needed. There has to be an employment policy, a policy of income redistribution and a policy of time — free time.

This is no small matter. For a policy of freeing time touches at one of the linchpins of the social order established nearly two centuries ago.

Work less, live more

'Work less, live more!' Since its birth, the labour movement has always struggled to reduce work time. Marx considered this to be the 'fundamental imperative'. May Day — the 'festival of labour' — originated as the culminating point of an international movement for the 'self-reduction' of working hours. Workers of the whole world were called upon by their trade unions to refuse to do more than eight hours a day from 1 May 1906. Three quarters of a century later, it is in the struggle to free time that the labour movement has made the least progress.

Table 2: *Who Works the Most?*

Total annual working hours

Great Britain	1932
France	1831
West Germany	1671
Holland	1626
Belgium	1545
Italy	1503

Average hours worked per week

Great Britain	
men	44.0
women	37.4
West Germany	42.0
Holland	41.0
Japan	40.7
France	40.6
Italy	38.9
Belgium	35.8

Source: *European Trade Union Research 1980.*

Yet, in the course of this century, productivity (i.e. output per hour of work) has risen twelvefold. Since 1936 and the law establishing a 40-hour week in France, it has almost quadrupled. But the number of working hours has not fallen noticeably. Is this because wage earners have preferred more money to more time? As we shall see, this is not so. The resistance has come from above: industrial societies — above all, management — have been fiercely opposed to the reduction of working hours. This may be seen in France today, as in Germany a few years ago. Generalisation of the 35-hour week has been denounced by French employers as a ruinous and exorbitant demand, as if yearly working hours in France were not among the highest in the industrialised world, as if the 40-hour week obtained 45 years ago corresponded to some inviolable law, as if the micro-electronic revolution were not in the process of eliminating jobs by the million, and as if the desire to live more were a sin and work frenzy a vital necessity.

Why does the right always prefer to reduce the number of workers in employment by 10 per cent rather than cut working hours by 10 per cent? There is little point in trying to find an economic answer to this question. For the free time imposed in the form of unemployment is much more costly than the time freed by a job-creating reduction in the working week.

The Arithmetic of Job Sharing

According to calculations carried out by the Commissariat Général du Plan at the request of the CFDT union federation, a 35-hour week without loss of earnings would make it possible to employ 850,000 more people than the 40-hour week can accommodate. There are, however, two conditions: plant and machinery must be used as inten-sively as they are at present; and wage differentials must be pro-gressively reduced.

According to a survey, rather than a calculation, carried out by CFDT officials in 578 departments of 350 enterprises, the implementa-tion of a 35-hour week would lead to a much greater increase in the workforce than economists have estimated. The increment would be distributed thus:

blue-collar workers	+ 8-10.8%
white-collar workers	+ 8-8.7%
technicians	+ 9.5%
middle management	+ 7.0%
upper management	+ 7.4%

The fundamental reasons for employers' hostility are of a quite different, essentially ideological order.

Imagine that society were to distribute yearly productivity gains in the following way: a third in the form of greater pur-chasing power, and two thirds in the form of additional free time. With an annual increase in productivity of 5 per cent — easily achieved in the past — the length of the working week would fall from 40 to 35 hours over a period of four years. After four more years it would stand at no more than 30½ hours, and after a total of 12 years would amount to 26 hours 40 minutes. A 20-hour week could be achieved in 20 years, by the year 2001;

and, if we take vacations and public holidays into account, would amount to a yearly total of barely 900 hours.

Now, 900 hours of work a year corresponds to two days' work a week over a year, or nine days' work a month, or five months' full-time work at today's rhythm followed by seven months free. This is not a great deal. 'Work' — or time exchanged for a wage — would then no longer be one's principal occupation. Everyone would — or could — define themselves with reference to their free time activities rather than their paid work.

What then would happen to the ethic of speed and punctuality, of 'we're not here for fun' — an ethic inculcated into children at school ever since the invention of manufactures? What would happen to the glorification of effort, speed and performance which is the basis of all industrial societies, capitalist or socialist? And if the ethic of performance collapsed, what would become of the social and industrial hierarchy? On what values and imperatives could those in command base their authority? Would they not have to treat wage earners as autonomous individuals, seeking their cooperation rather than demanding their obedience?

Millions of large and small bosses draw back in horror at this type of question. Instinctively they perceive the freeing of time as a threat to the established order. Instinctively they prefer higher unemployment to more free time. For unemployment is a disciplinary force. When jobs are scarce they can be kept for the most hard-working and submissive. Trouble-makers, militants and layabouts — they can remain without work. 'They're the unemployed,' it can then be said, 'and they've only themselves to blame. There's no room for wise guys any more.'

Thus the very same technological developments that make it possible to free time and reduce everyone's work load also allow the Right, through the weapon of unemployment, to reinforce the old ideology of hard work and productivity just when it no longer has any further economic or technical basis. Nowhere is the line separating Left and Right clearer than on the question of the social management of free time: on *the politics of time*. According to whether it is a politics (and policy) of the Right or the Left, it may lead either to a society based on unemployment or to one based on free time. Of all the levers available to change the social order and the quality of life, this is one of the most powerful.

In this connection, one should read or re-read an astonishingly rich study which sets forth the philosophy and objectives that a left-wing time policy will have to embrace. Produced by the *Échanges et Projets* group around Jacques Delors and edited by Laurence Cossé, the work is entitled *La Révolution du Temps Choisi* (*The Revolution of Choosing Your Time Schedule*, Paris, 1980.)

'The freeing of time,' they write,

> is a form of revolution or incitement to revolution insofar as it leads, almost automatically, to calling the productivist socio-cultural model into question... To a greater or lesser extent, all attempts to find an alternative model of development turn upon the question of time... Everything connected with ecology, decentralised sources of energy, conviviality, self-reliance, mutual aid and social experimentation is based upon different modes of managing time.

So time should be freed. But who will be the beneficiaries? Won't they consist largely of those who earn so much that they do not have time to spend their money, listen to their taped music, look at their videos and live in their country cottages? Isn't it true that the poor, who have always done the drudgery, are deprived of the cultural resources and facilities for leisure, and housed in concrete deserts where the only way to kill time is to yawn in front of a television set?

Delors's group both accepts and dismisses these objections. It accepts them by refusing to support a policy that sets out to grant and impose more free time on everyone through bureaucratic and legislative means. One should not be *given* more free time but empowered to *take* it. If people want to take it, this will be because they have 'suppressed plans' or aspirations which cannot be satisfied merely by the money they earn. It matters little whether they want to 'learn to play the lute or do yoga', build a house themselves or install a solar heating system, campaign in public affairs, set up a cooperative, work the land or spend more time with their children. The crucial point is that these activities should be self-defined and autonomously chosen, so that individuals are able to free themselves from the 'bureaucratic straitjacket' and 'those two vampires of the modern world: complexity and speed'. 'Individual autonomy begins when each individual can freely dispose of his or her time' — beginning at school.

Learning To Be Bored

'All the defects of the way we organise time are engraved in their purest form in school time. Between the ages of four and eighteen, children devote the majority of their time to learning.
  Already at school there is a 40-hour week. *Real life* is elsewhere.
  Time at school is soon excessively overloaded. Hours in the classroom are drab, slow and tiring — the child's counterpart to the tedium of work.
  It is time fragmented in the most ridiculous way: time spent learning and free time; school time and holidays.
  It is uniform time, which does violence to the obvious heterogeneity of naturally *unmoulded* children, and still more to their development, which, as all psychologists and biologists agree, is governed by different rhythms.
  Such education works to prevent the control of time. Indeed, the whole system is antithetic to the self-management of time.'

Source: La Révolution du Temps Choisi, *p.222.*

A policy of time cannot, however, be based solely upon individual choices. For, as Danièle Linhart has pointed out (*L'Appel de la sirène (l'accoutumance au travail)* Paris, Sycomore 1981) industrial society 'has created a vacuum around work', to such an extent that, in the eyes of the young workers whom Linhart interviewed, 'not going to work' could only mean 'staying at home and doing nothing'. The idea that there might be a thousand and one things to do outside the constraints of work does not tally with the experience of many people. The freeing of time therefore also requires collective decisions of a new type, 'an improvement in the social environment' and in the fabric of urban life, facilities that can be used and self-managed by individuals, neighbourhoods and small cooperatives. 'A policy of time implies a vision for society': it 'cannot be formulated without a patient, cumulative search for a new model of development'. There can be no policy of time which does not call for new cultural, education and urban policies, new industrial and work relations and so on.

This said, however, Delors and his group vigorously reject the argument that 'the masses are not ready' for more free time and will only be ready when the state — always the state — sets up institutions to take charge of people's leisure time. The 'organisation of leisure', where the (socialist or fascist) state dragoons the young and the old, men and women workers, mothers, school children etc into carefully separated activities, is worth no more than the leisure organised by the merchants of escapism.

'Between work constraints and alienating leisure, the politics of time seeks to open a new social space made up of experiment, authenticity and creativity.' The task is neither to change society and its institutions as a prior condition, nor to leave all social change to individuals alone. Rather, an overall policy should be fostered hand in hand with the thousand and one individual, community and cooperative initiatives that will fill the social space opened up by the freeing of time.

But if free time should not be 'granted or imposed', how should the matter be tackled? For the authors of *La Révolution du Temps Choisi*, the first necessity is to abolish compulsory working hours, *even at school*, 'so that each individual has real freedom to choose when he or she wants to work'. We need to 'get away from the universal productivist injunction', 'the system of prefabricated timetables'. 'Every wage earner must be given the possibility of reducing his or her own worktime (and pay); the employers should have the right to reject this only in a limited number of specifically defined and controlled circumstances.'

A utopia? A wild dream? Not at all. In Germany, at this present moment, 20 per cent of all employees freely choose the hours at which they begin and end work. It's a matter of organisation and self-organisation. In the Beck stores in Munich, employing 700 people, everyone is able to choose the monthly amount of work that suits them best. Their choices are reviewed each month at staff meetings, where employees monitor the situation and allocate days on by reconciling the needs of the job with each individual's preference. This is self-management of time — and of work, too. There is also a daily meeting with the departmental head to negotiate the required hours of attendance. Everything is possible, provided that someone volunteers to stand in for another person on unscheduled leave.

The right to sick leave has been preserved (this is not always the case in similar schemes in the United States). Each individual receives a monthly wage in proportion to the number of hours he or she has undertaken to put in, even if they are not all worked. Any shortfall can be made up when convenient, provided that everything balances out at the end of the year. Conversely, everyone is entitled to put in as many as 20 extra hours a month, later receiving them back in one or several lump-sum periods. Overtime does not exist.

How much time do the employees at Beck's choose to work? In 40 per cent of cases, it is less than the French legal norm of 173 hours a month. This is a relatively small proportion. It would be much higher if Beck's employees were subject to rigid timetables, as is the case elsewhere, instead of being able to choose and vary when to begin and end work. Indeed, according to a survey carried out in 1979 by the Nuremburg Employment Research Institute, 88 per cent of wage earners would prefer to work less, even if they thereby earn less.

This preference for time over money represents the most important cultural transformation of the current period. It has spread to every industrial nation.

Money Down

Would you prefer an increase in wages or in free time?

	wages	time
France	43%	57%
Europe as a whole	45%	55%

The percentages shown relate to the working population only.

Source: Opinion poll coordinated by IFOP in nine EEC states in 1977.

In ten years' time, thanks to technological progress, you could either earn twice as much or work half as much. What would be your preference?

Work half as much	63%
Earn twice as much	37%

The percentages indicate positive answers. The sample was representative of the French population as a whole, including those in retirement or not working. Thirteen per cent of the sample did not respond.

Source: Poll conducted for the Nouvel Observateur *by SOFRES, October 1978.*

Consumption, or the buying of goods and services, is ceasing to be the primary aspiration. After believing for over a century that 'time is money' or that nothing is worth more than the money earned by *selling one's time*, society is discovering that there are gratifications money cannot buy and which, on top of that, *cost nothing*. Wage labour is thus progressively ceasing to form the centre of people's lives. In Sweden, in the space of 22 years, the proportion of those reported to attach more importance to their work than their free time has fallen from 33 per cent to 17 per cent. In other words, the 'masses' have indeed given priority to freeing time.

'Of course,' conservatives of all persuasions will reply, 'this is because most people no longer have a real craft. They aren't interested in what they do. And you encourage them by saying that they have the right to think of their work as something peripheral to their lives.' This is why many feminists are hostile to 'part-time work'. In their eyes, it is incompatible with practising a 'true profession'.

The reality is very different. In France, part-time work is spreading most rapidly in the medical and teaching professions, and its enthusiasts argue that it is superior to full-time work in allowing them to update their knowledge and to devote much more care and attention to their work. Among the 16 per cent of Americans who have chosen to work less than 35 hours a week (mostly for less than 30 hours) there is no shortage of professionally qualified people working part-time within group practices and partnerships: lawyers, doctors, architects, industrial consultants, systems analysts, audit experts, and so on. The sharing of jobs by two or even three people is not confined to subordinate or marginal occupations. Stanford University in California has two part-time directors, as do the municipal services in Palo Alto. The New York Life Insurance Company has 240 policy writers for 120 jobs. The list of those working part-time in Germany includes the director of Hamburg's Health Department, numerous doctors working for sickness benefit schemes, and the director of the Munich underground. The latter, for example, works two and a half days a week and looks after his children and the house for the rest of the time, while his wife works (also part-time) as a town planner. This type of work-sharing scheme is much more widespread in the Scandinavian countries where the notions of a 'head of the family' and the sexual division of labour are tending to become obsolete.

The productivity of two people working part-time is generally much higher than that of one individual working full-time. Two people sharing a job are more open-minded, are never overloaded with work and, above all, provide a wider range of abilities and knowledge. The advantage to employers is such that certain firms in the USA and Germany tend to employ only part-time personnel. According to the University of Mannheim survey of 35 industrial enterprises in the Rhineland, a part-time worker's productivity is, on average, 33 per cent higher than that of a full-time worker. There is no reason why employers alone should benefit from these gains in productivity.

It should be noted in passing that if the same proportion of part-time workers existed in France as in Germany (14 per cent instead of 9 per cent), there would be 500,000 fewer unemployed.

But part-time work or a shorter working week are far from being the only, or the best, ways of freeing time. As average working time falls to 30, 25 and 20 hours a week, it will become essential to introduce even more flexible arrangements: for example, 'retirement advances' available at any age in return for an equivalent postponement of final retirement; 'sabbatical years' (one in seven) as given by universities and some American newspapers; or 'time savings-accounts', allowing people who have worked more in previous years to stop or reduce work for a year without loss of earnings.

Every conceivable formula presupposes what the Swedish economist Goesta Rehn has called a 'time bank': a social account of the number of hours worked which allows everyone to lend or borrow time from society while being guaranteed a lifelong minimum income. The only condition is that they should work a minimum number of hours in their active lifetime — a number which may obviously vary with technical progress or politico-economic choices. This brings us back to the idea of a guaranteed wage for life which, though demanded or obtained by American trade unions, cannot be made available to all within a free-market economy.

In the last few years, the idea of a guaranteed income for life has been discussed in all countries with an old social-democratic tradition. But its proponents no longer see it as a means of simply extending welfare state responsibility for the wellbeing of citizens. Indeed, it mainly stems from a recognition that, in the age of automation, the right to do work and receive an income must be clearly distinguished from the right to a *paid job*. This latter can no longer be guaranteed. It therefore has to be ensured that citizens can live and work without an employer to 'give' and buy their work. The key to a solution, we suspect, is to be found in cooperative and mutualist activities.

Every socialist party is currently interested in such schemes (which were part of the union movement at its beginnings). This revival of interest has been prompted by urgent practical reasons. The demand for social services and benefits has reached such a level that, in Northern Europe as a whole, state deductions are approaching — or already exceed — 50 per cent of GNP. At the same time, people are increasingly dissatisfied with the quality of institutionalised services. The problem facing socialists is no longer to extend state responsibility for citizens, but to improve the quality of services while reducing their scale and cost.

How is this to be done? The answer is that a radical attack should be made on the causes of the exploding demand for institutionalised services. These causes all come down to lack of time. Parents no longer have enough time for their children, nor the young for the old, the healthy for the sick or the able-bodied for the handicapped. As a result, babies are sent to day-care centres, the old to old-people's homes, the handicapped to special centres, 'maladjusted' pupils to special classes where they stagnate for ever, and so on.

In this way the fabric of interpersonal relations has been destroyed — to the benefit of bureaucratically provided 'services' which are both costly and eminently frustrating for their 'beneficiaries'. On top of this, neither men, women nor children have enough time to wash, clean, repair or mend things (assuming that they learned how to do so). Anything old is just thrown out. No one has the time to learn the arts of conviviality. Music, shows and games are not produced autonomously but bought in standardised form from the appropriate industries. No one has the time to cook, repaint or wallpaper rooms etc. All these activities are handed over in part or full to specialists, an hour of whose time costs you a great deal more than your own hourly pay.

All in all, at the level of society as well as the family, the lack of time means impoverishment and extra expenditure. We have barely begun to add up the 'hidden costs of productivism'. More time would make it possible to develop household as well as artistic, cultural and craft production; it would allow more direct involvement in running neighbourhoods or towns, and the creation of cooperative laundries, canteens, kitchen gardens, community repair workshops. Lastly, it would allow much cheaper and more satisfying services to be exchanged within the framework of the neighbourhood, housing estate or local cooperative.

Above all, the freeing of time through a free choice of working hours is the best and most rapid way of 'changing the quality of life' and, at the same time, of creating jobs. In the social and postal services, in local government, the hospitals and health-care centres, all that is needed is a simple ministerial directive to ensure that work in one's own freely chosen time becomes a reality. It is a fundamental reform that will cost practically nothing.

Appendix 2:

Utopia for a Possible Dual Society*

When they woke up that morning, the citizens asked themselves what new turmoil awaited them. After the elections, but during the period of transition to the new administration, a number of factories and enterprises had been taken over by the workers. The young unemployed, who for the previous two years had been occupying abandoned plants in order to engage in 'wildcat production' of various socially useful products, were now joined by a growing number of students, older workers who had been laid off recently, and retired people. In many places, empty buildings were being transformed into communes, production cooperatives, or 'alternative schools'. In the schools themselves the older pupils were taking the lead in practising skills for self-reliance and, with or without the collaboration of the teachers, establishing hydroponic gardens and facilities for raising fish and rabbits; in addition, students were beginning to install equipment for woodworking, metalworking, and other crafts which had for a long time been neglected or relegated to marginal institutions.

The day after the new government came into office, those who set out for work found a surprise awaiting them: during the night, in most of the large cities, white lines had been painted on all the major thoroughfares. Henceforth these would have a corridor reserved for buses, while on the sidestreets similar corridors were set aside for bicyclists and motorcyclists. At the major points of entry to each city, hundreds of bicycles and mopeds were assembled for use by the public, and long lines of police cars and army vans supplemented the buses. On this

---

* This appendix first appeared in André Gorz, *Ecology as Politics*, Boston, South End Press 1980.

morning, no tickets were being sold or required on the buses or suburban trains.

At noon, the government announced that it had reached the decision to institute free public transportation throughout the country, and to phase out, over the next 12 months, the use of private automobiles in the most congested urban areas. Seven hundred new tram-lines would be created or re-opened in the major metropolitan centres, and 26,000 new buses would be added to city fleets during the course of the year. The government also announced the immediate elimination of VAT on bicycles and small motorbikes, thus reducing their purchase price by 15 per cent.

That evening, the president of the Republic and the prime minister went on nationwide television to explain the larger design behind these measures. Since 1972, the president said, the GNP per person in France has reached a level close to that of the United States. 'Indeed, my fellow citizens,' the president concluded, 'we have nearly caught up with the US. But,' he added soberly, 'this is not something to be proud of.'

The president reminded his listeners of the period, not so distant, when the standard of living of Americans seemed an impossible dream to French people. Only ten years ago, he recalled, liberal politicians were saying that once the French worker began earning American wages, that would be the end of revolutionary protests and anti-capitalist movements. They had been, however, profoundly mistaken. A large proportion of French workers and employees were now receiving salaries comparable to those being paid in the US without this having diminished the level of radical activism. 'On the contrary. For in France, as in the United States, the people find themselves having to pay more and more to maintain an increasingly dubious kind of well-being. We are experiencing increasing costs for decreasing satisfactions. Economic growth has brought us neither greater equity nor greater social harmony and appreciation of life. I believe we have followed the wrong path and must now seek a new course.' Consequently, the government had developed a programme for 'an alternative pattern of growth, based on an alternative economy and alternative institutions'. The philosophy underlying this programme, the president stated, could be summed up in three basic points:

1. 'We shall work less.' Until now, the purpose of economic activity has been to amass capital in order to increase production and sales, and to create profits which, reinvested, would permit the accumulation of more capital, and so on. But this process must inevitably reach an impasse. Beyond a certain point, it could not continue unless it destroyed the surplus it had created. 'We have reached that point today,' the president said. 'It is, in fact, only by wasting our labour and our resources that we have managed in the past to create a semblance of full employment of people and productive capacities.'

In the future, therefore, it would be necessary to consider working less, more effectively, and in new ways. The president said that the prime minister would spell out the details of proposed measures for change in this direction. Without going into them, the president nevertheless stated that they would give substance to the following principle: 'Every individual will, as a matter of right, be entitled to the satisfaction of his or her needs, regardless of whether or not he or she has a job.' The president argued that once the productive machinery reaches the level of technical efficiency where a fraction of the available workforce can supply the needs of the entire population, it is no longer possible to make the right to a full income dependent on having a full-time job. 'We have earned,' the president concluded, 'the right to free work and to free time.'

2. 'We must consume better.' Until now products had been designed to produce the greatest profit for the firms selling them. 'Henceforth,' the president said, 'they will be designed to produce the greatest satisfaction for those who use them as well as for those who produce them.'

To this end, the dominant firms in each sector would become the property of society. The task of the great firms would be to produce, in each area, a restricted number of standardised products, of equal quality and in sufficient amounts, to satisfy the needs of all. The design of these products would be based on four fundamental criteria: durability, ease of repair, pleasantness of manufacture, and absence of polluting effects.

The durability of products, expressed in hours of use, would be required to appear alongside the price. 'We foresee a very strong foreign demand for these products,' the president added, 'for they will be unique in the world.'

3. 'We must re-integrate culture into the everyday life of all.' Until now, the extension of education had gone hand in hand with that of generalised incompetence.

Thus, said the president, we unlearned how to raise our own children, how to cook our own meals and make our own music. Paid technicians now provide our food, our music, and our ideas in prepackaged form. 'We have reached the point,' the president remarked, 'where parents consider that only state-certified professionals are qualified to raise their children adequately.' Having earned the right to leisure, we appoint professional buffoons to fill our emptiness with electronic entertainment, and content ourselves with complaining about the poor quality of the goods and services we consume.

It had become urgent, the president said, for individuals and communities to regain control over the organisation of their existence, over their relationships and their environment. 'The recovery and extension of individual and social autonomy is the only method of avoiding the dictatorship of the state.'

The president then turned to the prime minister for a statement of the new programme. The latter began by reading a list of 29 enterprises and corporations whose socialisation would be sought in the national assembly. More than half belonged to the consumer goods sector, in order to be able to give immediate application to the principles of 'working less' and 'consuming better'.

To translate these principles into practice, the prime minister said it was necessary to rely on the workers themselves. They would be free to hold general assemblies and set up specialised groups, following the system devised by the workers of Lip watch factory, where planning is done in specialised committees, but decisions are taken by the general assembly. The workers should allow themselves a month, the prime minister estimated, to define, with the assistance of outside advisers and consumer groups, a reduced range of product models and new sets of quality standards and production targets. New management systems had already been devised by a semi-clandestine group of ministry of finance officials.

During this first month, said the prime minister, production work should be done only in the afternoons, the mornings being reserved for collective discussion. The workers should set as their goal the organising of the productive process to meet the demands for essential goods, while at the same time reducing their average work time to 24 hours a week. The number of workers would evidently have to be increased. There would, he promised, be no shortage of women and men ready to take these jobs.

The prime minister further remarked that the workers would be free to organise themselves in such a way that each individual could, for certain periods, work more or less than the standard 24 hours for the same firm. They would be free to have two or three part-time jobs or, for example, to work on construction during the spring and in agriculture towards the end of the summer — in short, to learn and practise a variety of skills and occupations. To facilitate this process, the workers themselves would be helped to set up a system of job exchanges, taking into account that the 24-hour week, and the monthly salary of £400 to which they would be entitled, should be regarded as an average.

Two people, said the prime minister, should be able to live quite comfortably on £400 a month, considering the range of collective services and facilities which would be available to them. But no one need feel restrained by this: 'Luxuries will not be prohibited. But they must be obtained by additional work.' As examples, the prime minister cited the following: a second residence or summer cottage represented about 3000 hours of labour. Anyone seeking to acquire one would work, in addition to the 24 hours a week, 3000 hours in the building and construction sector, of which at least 1000 hours would need to be completed before a loan could be raised. Other objects classified as non-necessities, such as private automobiles (which represented about 600 hours of labour), could be acquired in the same fashion. 'Money itself will no longer confer any rights,' the Prime Minister stated. 'We must learn to determine the prices of things in working hours.' This labour-cost, he added, would rapidly decline. Thus the individual with some do-it-yourself skills would soon be able to acquire, for only 500 hours of additional work, all the elements needed to assemble his or her own house, which should not take more than 1500 hours to put up.

The government's economic aim, the prime minister stated, was to gradually eliminate commodity production and exchange by decentralising and scaling down production units in such a way that each community was able to meet at least half of its needs. The source of the waste and frustration of modern life, the prime minister noted, was that 'no one consumes what he or she produces and no one produces what he or she consumes'.

As a first step in the new direction, the government had negotiated with the bicycle industry an immediate 30 per cent increase in production, but with at least half of all the bicycles and motorcycles being provided as kits to be put together by the users themselves. Detailed instruction sheets had been printed, and assembly shops with all the necessary tools would be installed without delay in town halls, schools, police stations, army barracks, and in parks and car parks.

The prime minister voiced the hope that in the future local communities would develop this kind of initiative themselves: each neighbourhood, each town, indeed each block of flats, should set up studios and workshops for free creative work and production; places where people could produce whatever they wished during their free time, thanks to the increasingly sophisticated array of tools they would find at their disposal (including stereo equipment or closed-circuit television). The 24-hour week and the fact that income would no longer depend on holding a job would permit people to organise so as to create neighbourhood services (caring for children, helping the old and the sick, teaching each other new skills) on a cooperative or mutual-aid basis, and to install convenient neighbourhood facilities and equipment. 'Stop asking, whenever you have a problem, "What is the government doing about it?" ' the prime minister exclaimed. 'The government's vocation is to abdicate into the hands of the people.'

The cornerstone of the new society, the prime minister continued, was the rethinking of education. It was essential that, as part of their schooling, all young people learn to cultivate the soil, to work with metal, wood, fabrics and stone, and that they learn history, science, mathematics and literature in conjunction with these activities.

After completing compulsory education, the prime minister went on, each individual would be required to put in 20 hours of work each week (for which he or she would earn a full salary), in addition to continuing with whatever studies or training he or she desired. The required social labour would be done in one or more of the four main sectors: agriculture, mining and steelworks; construction and public works; public hygiene; and care of the sick, the aged and children.

The prime minister specified that no student-worker would, however, have to perform the most disagreeable jobs, such as collecting rubbish, being a nurse's aide, or doing maintenance work, for more than three months at a time. Conversely, everyone up to the age of 45 would be expected to perform these tasks for an average of 12 days a year (12 days a year would mean one day per month or one hour per week). 'There will be neither nabobs nor pariahs in this country any more,' the prime minister remarked. In a matter of two years, 600 multi-disciplinary centres of self-learning and self-teaching, open day and night, would be put within easy reach of everyone, even of people living in rural areas, so that no one would be imprisoned in a menial occupation against his or her choice.

The student-workers would also be expected, during their last year of work-education, to organise themselves into small autonomous groups to design and carry out an original initiative of some kind, which would be discussed beforehand with the local community. The prime minister expressed the hope that many of these initiatives would seek to give new life to the declining rural regions of France, and serve to reintroduce agricultural practices more in harmony with the ecosystem. Many people were unduly worried by the fact that France depends on foreign sources of gasoline and industrial fuel, when it was far more serious to be dependent on American soybean meal to raise beef, or on petrochemical fertilisers to grow grains and vegetables.

'Defending our territory,' the prime minister said, 'requires first of all that we occupy it. National sovereignty depends first of all on our capacity to grow our own food.' For this reason the government would do everything possible to encourage 100,000 people a year to establish themselves in the depopulated regions of the country, and to reintroduce and improve organic farming methods and other 'soft' technologies. All necessary scientific and technical assistance would be provided free for five years to newly established rural communities. This would do more to overcome world hunger than the export of nuclear power stations or insecticide factories.

The prime minister concluded by saying that, in order to encourage the exercise of imagination and the greater exchange of ideas, no television programmes would be broadcast on Fridays and Saturdays.

Andre Gorz

Ecology as Politics

Ecology as Politics is an examination of the relationship between ecological balance and our economic and political structures.
An earlier critique of social development than *Farewell to the Working Class*, Gorz argues for the need for fighters for democratic socialism and an ecological society to address their mutual values and aims.
'Socialism is no better than capitalism if it makes use of the same tools. The total domination of nature inevitably entails a domination of people by the techniques of domination.'

0 86104 904 7   paperback

Stephen Shalom (Editor)

Socialist Visions

What does the left mean when it advocates 'socialism' for the United
States? Six major essays provocatively describe different aspects of a
socialist America: politics, the family and sex roles, race and
nationalism, the built environment, economics, the division of labour.
Thirteen respondents, including Michael Harrington and Jeremy
Brecher, add to the discussion from a number of viewpoints. Their
exchanges with the authors create a dialogue on the meaning of
socialism that is both exciting and visionary.

0 86104 719 2   paperback

Pluto books are available through your local bookshop. In case of
difficulty contact Pluto to find out local stockists or to obtain
catalogues/leaflets.
If all else fails write to:

Pluto Press Limited

The Works
105A, Torriano Avenue
London NW5 1YP

To order, enclose a cheque/p.o. payable to Pluto Press to cover price
of book, plus 50p per book for postage and packing (£2.50
maximum).